AYURVEDA
PERFECT HEALTH

AYURVEDA FOR PERFECT HEALTH

PROF. T.L. DEVARAJ

UBSPD®
UBS Publishers' Distributors Pvt. Ltd.
New Delhi • Bangalore • Kolkata • Chennai • Patna • Bhopal
Ernakulam • Mumbai • Lucknow • Pune • Hyderabad

UBS Publishers' Distributors Pvt. Ltd.

5 Ansari Road, New Delhi-110 002
Phones: 011-23273601-4, 23266646-47, 23274846, 23282281, 23273552
Fax: 23276593, 23274261• E-mail: ubspd@ubspd.com

10 First Main Road, Gandhi Nagar, Bangalore-560 009
Phones: 080-22253903, 22263901, 22263902, 22255153 • Fax: 22263904
E-mail: ubspd@bngm.ubspd.com, ubspdbng@airtelbroadband.in

8/1-B Chowringhee Lane, Kolkata-700 016
Phones: 033-22529473, 22521821, 22522910 • Fax: 22523027
E-mail: ubspdcal@cal.ubspd.com

60 Nelson Manickam Road, Aminjikarai, Chennai-600 029
Phones: 044-23746222, 23746351-2 • Fax: 23746287
E-mail: dbs@che.ubspd.com,ubspdche@che.ubspd.com

Ground Floor, Annapurna Complex, Naya Tola, Patna-800 004
Phones: 0612-2672856, 2673973, 2686170 • Fax: 2686169
E-mail: ubspdpat@pat.ubspd.com

Z-18, M.P. Nagar, Zone-I, Bhopal-462 011
Phones: 0755-4203183, 4203193, 2555228 • Fax: 2555285
E-mail: ubspdbhp@bhp.ubspd.com

No. 40/7940-41, Kollemparambil Chambers, Convent Road, Ernakulam-682 035
Phones: 0484-2353901, 2363905 • Fax: 2365511
E-mail: ubspdekm@ekm.ubspd.com

2nd Floor, Apeejay Chambers, 5 Wallace Street, Fort, Mumbai-400 001
Phones: 022-66376922, 66376923, 66102067, 66102069
Fax: 66376921 • E-mail: ubspdmum@mum.ubspd.com

9, Ashok Nagar, Near Pratibha Press, Gautam Buddha Marg, Latouche Road,
Lucknow-226 018 • Phones: 4025124, 4025134, 4025144, 6531753
Fax 4025144 • Email: ubspdlko@lko.ubspd.com

680 Budhwar Peth, 2nd floor, Near Appa Balwant Chowk, Pune-411 002
Phone: 020-24461653 • Fax: 020-24433976 • E-mail:
ubspdpune@pun.ubspd.com

NVK Towers, 2nd floor, 3-6-272/B, Himayat Nagar, Hyderabad-500 029
Phones: 040-23262572, 23262573, 23262574
Fax: 040-23262572 • E-mail: ubspdhyd@hyd.ubspd.com

Visit us at www.ubspd.com & www.gobookshopping.com

© Prof. T.L. Devaraj

First Published	2002
First Reprint	2004
Second Reprint	2007

Prof. T.L. Devaraj asserts the moral right
to be identified as the author of this work.

Illustrations: UBS Art Studio

Printed at: Pauls Press, Delhi

Dedicated to
Late Rajamantra Praveena, Shri H B Gundappa Gowda
Hon. Minister for Local Self-Government
and Public Health
The then Govt. of Mysore
who was a pioneer in starting several Ayurvedic
dispensaries and hospitals in the state

Justice H.G. Balakrishna
Former Judge
High Court of Karnataka

774, 15th Cross
J.P. Nagar 1st Phase
Bangalore-560 078
Phone: 6630935

FOREWORD

Dr. T.L. Devaraj has done a highly commendable job in bringing out his twenty-second book on Ayurveda bringing to bear his vast experience and knowledge for the benefit of the people and society. As the dictum goes, knowledge is the horse and experience is the rider.

This book bearing the title, *Ayurveda for Perfect Health* is elegant and simple in style. It is articulate and intelligible enough even for a layman. The contents of the book are illuminating both in respect of the preventive aspect and the remedial factors. The book has global relevance particularly since Ayurvedic medicine has no side-effects unlike its allopathic counter-part.

As the author has pointed out, Ayurveda has unique ways of treatment apart from herbal remedies, mineral preparations and the body-cleansing therapies which detoxify the human body. Ayurvedic treatment assures both physical and mental equilibrium besides psychic soothing.

This invaluable book unfolds the glory of Ayurveda in all its dimensions and offers a perfect guide to everyone who wishes to reap the benefits of this ancient science which symbolises the inseparable and indispensable relations between nature and human beings. I hope that Dr. T.L. Devaraj continues his noble mission of perpetuating traditional Ayurveda with more and more contributions for the benefit of humanity.

I am happy that the learned author is dedicating this book to my father, late Rajamantrapravina H.B. Gundappa Gowda who took special interest in promoting and encouraging both Ayurvedic and Unani systems of medicines.

ACKNOWLEDGEMENTS

I wish to offer my gratitude

1. To Rajamantra Praveena, Late Shri H B Gundappa Gowda: dedicated for his Yeoman service to Ayurveda.
2. To Justice H.G. Balakrishna, former Judge, High Court of Karnataka—dedicated for his valuable foreword.
3. To my family for their encouragement.
4. To Mr. Balaram Sahu, Managing Director of U.B.S Bangalore, for his help in getting this book printed by UBS.
5. To my colleagues Dr. Sumithra Gowda and Dr. Sridhar, lecturers at Government Ayurveda Medical College, Bangalore, for having supplied books to me from their library.
6. To my friend Mr. H.T. Govinde Gowda, sub-divisional engineer, Telecom, Bangalore Division, and his family members for their moral support.
7. To all the authors and publishers of the books listed in Bibliography.
8. To all the sages of Ayurveda, who have done a yeoman service to humanity through Ayurveda.
9. To Mr. and Mrs. Manoj Garg, Bangalore, for their neat DTP work of this book.
10. To Mr. Govinda Rao, yoga specialist and his staff for having supplied photographs on Ayurveda exercises (yoga).

AUTHOR'S NOTE

The quest for good health is an incessant urge of all human beings. In this endeavour, they try to explore all possible avenues in search of health promoting food, exercise and meditation. Ayurveda is a science of life. It deals with the maintenance of physical, mental and social health of an individual as well as the society. It aims at not only the preventive aspect of the disease but also its curative nature. Ayurveda has laid major emphasis on man's psychosomatic constitution. It also lays more emphasis on personal hygiene that keeps one in sound health through the balance of basic components as Vata, Pitta and Kapha, throughout life.

The specific diet, exercise, sleep and meditation for each constitution are emphasised. One man's food is another man's poison. The treatment is also like that. One man's medicine is another man's poison. Ayurveda has unique ways of treatment, apart from herbal remedies, mineral preparations, and the body cleansing therapies-detoxifying the body. This is done by opening gateways of channels of healing and to tone up the system, the 'rasayana' or rejuvinative procedures and Ayurvedic exercise such as yoga for *vata*, *pitta* and *kapha* constitution and so on. The main purpose is to bring the imbalance of the 'doshas' to balance. The mental imbalance can be corrected through meditation. Aggravated 'rajas' and 'tamas' must be brought in to balance of satva guna through meditation and different types of therapies—music, primordial, sounds, gandharava music therapies and so on.

The perfect balance of somatic (body) and psycho (mind) can be achieved following the principles of Ayurveda, practice of principles of Ayurveda.

I have made a humble attempt in bringing to the world the glory of Ayurveda and its golden rules of the health of body and mind to promote perfect health in an individual. I hope students of Ayurveda and the public at large will derive maximum benefit from this work and pave the way for acquiring perfect health and live long.

Part-A
ATTAINING PERFECT HEALTH: INVITATION TO AYURVEDA FOR PERFECT HEALTH

Invitation to Ayurveda for perfect health is discussed with full details. In this part the possibility and feasibility of perfect health is also dealt with. Ayurveda postulates that man is homologous in nature, a microcosm of macrocosm universe, and is a photo print of nature. It is in the form of prakriti or constitution. In the second chapter, exploring of body types which are necessary for reaching highest goal of state of health, the perfect health is also explained. In this, one can find which type of body constitution he belongs to. Balancing of *doshas* is also essential for perfect health. The human body can maintain its balance with proper food, Ayurvedic exercises and meditation techniques. The suitable diet for each constitution is explained.

Part-B
QUANTUM BODY, MIND AND MEDICINE

This section deals with quantum body, mind and medicine. The mind acts on health and disease at the quantum level. The relationship of the body and mind was described in Ayurveda more than five thousand years ago. This takes place at the higher level of awareness of mind, which influences the physical body. This is more potent than medicine, diet or exercise.

In opening of the main gates of the channels of healing, the punchakarma-pentad of purificatory procedures meant for detoxifying the body and the mental toxins are removed through meditation, primordial aroma and Gandharva music therapy and so on.

One can live long and in good health by biding goodbye to addictions such as alcohol, smoking, drinking of soft drinks and coffee and tea. Premature ageing can be avoided by proper food, Ayurvedic exercises and a disciplined life.

Part-C
TRY TO LIVE WITH NATURE

Ayurveda advocates that everything one eats, thinks and drinks must be balanced. It is not at all possible at a glance but could be minimised to some extent by trying to live with nature. When a person is healthy in order to secure perfect health he should make little adjustment and adaptation of the rules and obeying the rules of nature as daily regimen, seasonal regimen, with these the imbalance doshas can be brought in to balance. The majority of imbalances could be prevented and the health of the body and mind is protected and preserved so as to attain the perfect health.

The balance could be at the physical, mental and also at the spiritual level. This has been told in Ayurveda so one has to make up to live in tune with nature. The balance must take place first at the quantum level. For this, the balance of digestive fire, body types of food of different tastes and proper Ayurvedic exercises must be adhered to. The irregularity in food intake leads to improper digestion and most of the diseases are due to this. Addictions like drinking and smoking lead to ill-health.

Mahashivarathri   **Prof. T.L. Devaraj**
4 March 2002
Bangalore

CONTENTS

Part A
Attaining Perfect Health: Invitation to
Ayurveda for Perfect Health

Part A

**Attaining Perfect Health: Invitation
to Ayurveda for Perfect Health**

Chapter One

ATTAINING PERFECT HEALTH: INVITATION TO AYURVEDA FOR PERFECT HEALTH

Perfect health is defined as a state where a person is physically and mentally free from disease and suffers no pain and he cannot grow old early or die early. In order to secure this, it may take either months or years. Ayurveda helps in promoting and procuring perfect health. *Ayurveda* is the science of life. The science of selfhealing. It is an *upaveda* of *Atharveda*. It is bestowed upon us by ancient seers, who were selfless and wise. They acquired eminence in the field of Ayurveda and possessed an insight in to our being and culture of the land. This is blessed with rich vegetation all over the world especially in India. Ayurveda is more suited not only to India, but also to the world at large. Most of the civilized world thinks, that they are supersonic in thought and action and also in their life style. Countries like Japan and America have shown keen interest and have scientific outlook for herbal system of medicine and treatment. We live with plants and we grow with them. These countries are already patronising Ayurveda.

It is necessary for the world, if not India, to make a national system of medicine incorporating the best out of ancient Ayurveda. The main object of Ayurveda is to protect health of the healthy persons and to alleviate the disorders of the diseased.

Ayurveda has stood the test of time, as it strikes directly at the pathogenesis of the disease. There are many diseases, which are not amenable to other systems of medicine. Ayurveda provides an answer for this. One has to read and adhere to the rules of health, types of body, food and regimen, which leads to a healthy life.

Ayurveda works at the quantum level of the body. Ayurveda has doctrines and its postulation, which are similar to nature, because the body is microcosm of the macrocosm of the universe. After visiting a new place, you come back feeling refreshed and energetic leading to definite changes in the body and mind.

The causative factors are mostly due to changes in our diet, activities and sleep. From the modern angle, the disease is caused by virus, bacteria, fungi and allergies. There are many organisms in the alimentary tract that do not cause any disease. But, in some people, these organisms become virulent and produce diseases. Some heart patients die immediately, while others live long. Man is host to many pathogenic organisms, but in some they keep quiet. Science does not give any answer for this eccentric activity. Ayurveda, however, gives the answer.

This is due to the fact that each one of us has got immunity. It is a defensive present in an individual. People who harbour mycobacterium tuberculosis may not get tuberculosis. But some patients with less resistance and less phagocytic action will get tuberculosis. Phagocytic action involves white blood cells. They engulf the organisms and digest them. When this activity fails in the body, the disease emerges.

Ayus means life and Veda is knowledge. So Ayurveda is knowledge of life which is as old as five thousand years. Ayurveda teaches how to attain good spiritual, mental and physical health.

Ayurveda has advocated opening the gateways of channel of quantum human body and also to detoxify the body and bring it back to normal state. The word quantum comes from physics. This body is the root cause of many cells, organs, thoughts, excitements, emotion, happiness and sorrow. As soon as the tongue comes in contact with food, it sends message to the brain to know the type of taste.

Nature has created the world of herbs, mountains, rocks, trees, animals, stars including sun and moon. Human body is more complex than all these, as it has been given a special organ—mind with brain. One can sit in India and at the same time can visualise through his mind, America or any the part of the world. It has a special sense of differentiation, of good from the bad, sorrow from happiness and so on.

Modern people suffer more from cancer, heart disease, arthritis, arteriosclerosis, diabetes, high blood pressure and so on.

These are the result of our behaviour, improper diet, untimely meals, smoking and excessive drinking of alcohol. A large sum of money is being spent all over the world for simply knowing the cause and to treat them effectively. Ayurveda advocates more preventive measures than curative ones as prevention is better than cure.

Ayurveda advocates discipline i.e. diurnal regimen, seasonal regimen, exercise, sleep and proper diet. All these are very important to prevent diseases. Exercise is recommended to prevent obesity, diabetes, high blood pressure and heart attacks.

The use of garlic in diet prevents rheumatism and high cholesterol. The use of turmeric, green gram and *Amalaki*, prevents diabetes. The use of cumin seeds in diet pacifies the *pitta* in the body. The use of pure honey pacifies the *kapha*. The use of til (sesame oil) works as *antivata*. Ayurveda hits at the very root of the disease. Orange prevents heart attacks by preventing clotting of blood and horsemilk dissolves blood clots.

Meditation keeps the mind in tranquility and hence, most of the psychic disorders, insanity, epilepsy and insomnia will not occur. The food that we take will give a sense of satisfaction to the brain through the nervous system.

The quantum of our body remains active though intelligence may be in the cells level depending on the changes that take place in tissues, muscles, nerves, arteries and in the brain cells.

Ayurveda pleads that the nature of our body is so minute that it can be pierced by the intelligence of the systems. Quantum changes can create changes in the physical body. To quote an example, if an insect bites a person he will get eruptions and pruritis. But another person will not be affected, because he has got enough resistance to allergic reactions. Physics says that molecules control the higher centres. The same thing holds good in our body. Skin becomes new in one month and eight days. The bone will become new in ninety days. The chemicals in the body, carbondioxide, oxygen, hydrogen, nitrogen will be new in few weeks. The fat in body is changed every three weeks and mucous membrane of the stomach every 4-5 weeks. The bone structures are replaced one in 2-3 months. So, Ayurveda can put up a better health care from the level of the quantum and it acts as perfect natural system of medicine for the entire world.

WHO has also recognised this system of medicine for securing perfect health.

Ayurveda preaches and practices that perfect health is secured through a balanced diet. The body is not very different from nature. The body will balance itself with little efforts from our side. The imbalance of the body is disease.

When a person is free from disease, experiences no pain and cannot grow old or die it is perfect health. In order to secure this, it may take months or years. This cause of disease is different in every individual.

For acquiring perfect health, it is necessary to update healthy individuals with 5 to 10 per cent of improvements in physical and mental aspects. This is possible only when a person is treated at quantum level. The quantum is nothing, but a basic unit if either matter or energy. It is 10,000,000 smaller than the tiniest atom. These are invisible vibrations. It holds good in human beings in order to make your health 5-10 times better. Ayurveda highlights the role of *swasthavritta* the rules of health, and diurnal routines and seasonal routines. Ayurveda concentrates on the involvement of mind, as it controls the entire body. The quantum human body is acted upon by the mind in its quantum level. Our bodily organs, tissues, cells and atoms are being influenced by the quantum status of the mind. The vibrations are also going on in the quantum level in the nervous systems. Whenever we consume food, the taste buds present in the tongue will act in the quantum level and transmit the information to the brain, in its quantum level and then you feel it is sweet, bitter, astringent. The tastes will trigger central and other nervous systems in their activity. The intellectual media that takes place in quantum level in the mind and has got enormous influences on the quantum of the body. The cell tissues and organs can be changed in their activity in a matter of seconds. A cancer patient who starts meditation twice in a day will influence the brain and it increases bodily resistance. This has to lead to a cure of cancer. So, Ayurveda and its doctrines have a say in promoting perfect health in a person. This takes place at the quantum level in mind and body system. It is new aspect of medicine.

Chapter Two

EXPLORE YOUR BODY TYPES

It is necessary to know your body type in order to determine the type of food one should take. No two persons are similar. Modern medicine is administered equally to all the people, irrespective of their body types. Hence the treatment is not always successful.

INTIAL STEP

Know your body type. We are in the habit of taking food, air and water according to the dictates of our internal tendencies. We cannot go against these, but we can modify them to some extent. Ayurveda advises us to live according to the tune of nature to be happy and without any stress.

Milk is full of proteins. For some it is good for growing bones, but for others it creates calculic (stones) in kidney. Ayurveda postulates the body types and recommends the types of food and exercise. In some countries people eat pork (pig meat) which consists of excessive fat. This fat increases arteriosclerosis, which is thickening of inner walls of the arteries causing obstruction of blood flow. Lack of blood supply to the heart leads to heart failure. In some people it does not occur. The disease takes root early and the external signs appear only at a later stage. Excess of fat and lack of exercise can lead to blocked arteries and cause heart attack.

ROLE OF BODY TYPES HELPS IN
PREVENTION OF DISEASE

Urban people suffer from heart disease, cancer, osteoporosis, spondylitis of the neck bone and vertebras. But, generally the poor people are not at all prone to these diseases.

These are degenerative diseases not amenable to modern methods of treatment. Diabetes, heart attacks and cancer occur in a particular type of people. People with *Kapha* constitution are prone to diabetes. So the predisposing factors are to be avoided to prevent the disease. Body types help in giving perfect and specific treatment to diseases.

Mr. Thimmaiah is suffering from stomach ulcer. The medicines prescribed for him are not the same for others, as he belongs to *Vata prakriti*. The food of *Vata prakriti* is different from those who are either *Pitta prakriti* or *Kapha prakriti*. So, in Ayurveda, body types help in pinpointing the diseases and the correct diet for curing them.

For people with *Pitta prakriti* and *Kapha prakriti* it is not good to consume soft drinks. It irritates the gastric mucosa and produces gastritis. Drinking coffee or tea on an empty stomach is also not good, as it overstimulates acid secretion resulting in ulcer formation. Hence, it is better to avoid these habits once for all for preventing disease and to get good health. *Prakriti* includes both mind and body.

THE BODY'S MAIN SWITCHING CENTRE

The dissimilarities between two persons are mainly due to three important principles called *doshas*. These *doshas* are important as they link the mind and body. The *doshas* when aggravated or imbalanced will disconnect the connection between mind and body. The three *doshas* are called Vata, Pitta and Kapha and they regulate several thousands different functions in the mind and body.

VATA DOSHA

A nervous phenomena which controls all the movement of the body including cells and quantum of the body.

PITTA DOSHA

It controls the digestive fire and internal secretions of endocrine glands.

KAPHA DOSHA

Mainly controls the structure of the body including cells, tissues and their quantum of the body. Every quantum of the body must have these three *doshas*. A person should have *vata dosha* which controls the respiration, heart rate, circulation of the blood and aids in digestion and sends impulses to the brain. The *pitta dosha* is nothing but digestive fire which regulates food digestion and maintenance of water and air in the entire body. The *kapha dosha* is necessary to hold each part of the cell or organs together like muscle, fat and bone. So finally, all three basic principles (three *doshas* are very necessary to make a human body). When an Ayurvedic practitioner declares you belong to *vata* constitution, then you have more predominant constitution as *vata,* in addition to other two *doshas* in minimum level.

The very aim of knowing *prakriti* is to adjust your food, exercise, daily regimen and seasonal routine and other factors necessary for preventing diseases. It is quite certain that our body is made up of three *doshas,* but it is said one *prakriti* depends upon the predominance of constitutional factors.

Take the example of a person waiting for a delayed plane at an airport. A person with *Vata prakriti* will get anxious, restless and impatient and will go to the concerned person and demand a refund.

A person with *Pitta* constitution will become angry and start criticising the authorities for the delay. But a person of *Kapha prakriti* will become lethargic and stay patiently, without a second thought.

HONOUR YOUR BODY TYPE OF CONSTITUTION

If one wants to be healthy, he should honour his body type of constitution. When one adjusts his food and activities with a balanced body and mind, then he will be in a state of balanced health. The *doshas*, the digestive fire, tissues and excreta are of balanced state is nothing but a state of perfect health that a person is of *vata* constitution he is simply and basically of *vata* predominant constitution. Everybody naturally will be with three constitutions but the predominance of constitution will decide and named as Vataja or Pittaja and Kaphaja constitution.

VATA CONSTITUTION (VATA PRAKRITI)

Vata period is the last one third of life (61 years to end of life).

The person with *vata* constitution has a flat chest, is physically lean and very active. Muscles, tendons and veins are distinctly seen outside. The complexion of the person is either brown or bluish. His skin will be rough, cold, dry and cracked. Dark curly hairs and with less muscles are prominent. Eyes will be small, dry and sunken and his conjunctiva will be muddy and dry. The digestion will differ from individual to individual and sometimes, it is variable. He likes sweet, sour and salt-tasted foods and he likes hot foods.

His faeces will be hard, dry and small in quantity. In the majority of cases he will be constipated. His sleep will be disturbed. His hands and feet are often cold and will be less prone to perspiration.

He talks and walks very fast and feels exhausted. He has a short memory due to intolerance and less confidence.

PITTA CONSTITUTION (PITTA PRAKRITI)

The person with *pitta* constitution has the following salient features:

Height	Medium
Body frame	Delicate
Chest	Medium
Muscles, Veins	Medium
Tendons	Medium prominence
Moles	Many, bluish or brownish
Skin	Warm, soft, less wrinkled
Hair	Thin, red, silky, early greying
Eyes	Medium prominence

Physiologically

Metabolism	Good
Digestion	Good
Appetite	Good, takes more food and liquids
Tastes	Sweets, bitter and astringent
Sleep	Uninterrupted
Body	Temperature higher than *vata*
Perspiration	More
Feet and hands	Warm
Tolerance	Heat and sun
Finance/Wealth	Enjoyed by *pitta* constitution.

The *pitta* period is the second one-third of life (31-60 years).

KAPHA CONSTITUTION (KAPHA PRAKRITI)

Body	Well developed
Weight	Excess
Chest	Broad and expanded
Veins, Muscles, Tendons	Not visible
Complexions	Bright and fair
Skin	Soft, oily and lustrous cold and pale
Hairs	Blue or black and dense and white and attractive

Physiologically

He will have the symptoms as stated under:

Appetite	Regular
Digestion	Slow
Quantity	Less
Tastes	Demand pungent, bitter and astringent
Life	Happy, healthy and quite peaceful
Mental	Loving, tolerant, calm, forgiving, greediness, hatred
Memory	Good
Finance	Wealthy and maintains it.

Kapha periods is from first one-third of life (up to 30 years).

A person Mr. Albert working in hot furnace factory came to me with a history of burning sensation all over the body with increase of blood pressure (Hypertension), red patches of the skin and sleeplessness. He said that he could not go to work. He was convinced to leave the job and opt for another one in the interest of protecting and preserving good health. Later, he did it and his health was restored to normal. This shows that *pitta* was aggravated during his working period and *pitta* disorders like hypertension and patches in the skin got started.

Balancing the *pitta* means balancing the mind and body systems. Mr. Albert did not need any medicines.

Prakriti means natural form of constitution. Ayurveda advocates the examination of a person for his constitution before diagnosis of diseases for treatment. There are two important *prakritis viz.* 1. *Dehaprakriti* (Body constitution) 2. *Manasik Prakriti* (Psychic constitution).

Now we deal with them one by one.

1. Physical constitution

(a) *Vata* constitution (b) *Pitta* constitution. (c) *Kapha* constitution. (d) *Vata pitta* constitution. (e) *Vata kapha* constitution, (f) *Pitta kapha* constitution, (g) *sama vata pitta kapha* constitution.

2. Psychic Constitution

In *Manasik prakriti* there are three psychic *doshas*. They are (a) *Satva*, (b) Rajas, (c) *Tamas*.

Usually *satvic* type of constitution will not produce any psychic deterioration or upsets.

ORIGIN OF PRAKRITI

The constitution of an individual is formed in five ways:

1. Shukra and Shonita

The *shukra* (semen) and the *shonita* (ovum) is determined depending on the predominant *doshas* at the time of conception of semen and ovum. The *beejabhagya*, double gene, DNA hereditary factor produces similar body complexion, voice, eyes, leanness or fatty body. This also notifies immunity to different types of *micro-organisms*. In Ayurveda this is called semenova consititution.

2. Kala garbhashaya constitution

Kala is defined as time and *garbhashya* is uterus. The role of uterus at the time of conception (semen and ova union) plays an important part in conception and much depends on the predominant *doshas* such as *Vata, Pitta* and *Kapha* and psychic, dominant *doshas satva, rajas,* and *tamas* of the mother.

3. Matru Aharavihara

The diet and activies of the mother during pregnancy plays a definite role in the composition of constitution of the body of the child.

4. Compatibility of Couple

Only if the couple is at peace mentally and both of them are of different clans(*gothras*)will a healthy child be born.

5. Mahabhuta Vikara

The *panchamahabutas*: Pentad of five elements also have a definite say in the formation of the constitution, including the father and mother factors, nutrients and *atma*.

COMBINED DOSHA PRAKRITIS

The combined *dosha* constitution is formed depending on the dominant *doshas* either qualitative or quantitative at the time of conception of semen and ovum in the uterus. The constitution is assessed depending upon the predominance of signs and symptoms of body *doshas* and psychic *doshas*.

The predominance of the *doshas* is necessary to aid the constitution—eye redness is due to *pitta*, whiteness is due to *kapha* and dryness is due to *vata*. Depending upon the presence of any one of these symptoms, the constitutional factors will be determined.

The constitution is determined usually by questioning the individual and also depending on the physical examination of the patient. Section 'A' deals with the interrogatory method. The marks depend on the answers for each question. Section B deals with physical examination. The assessment of marks for this is also done in the similar manner.

HOW TO DETECT YOUR CONSTITUTION

Go on calculating the marks for *vata, pitta* and *kapha* and count the total marks in each *dosha*. If *vata dosha* is more in count and *pitta dosha* and *kapha* come next then you have to come to conclusion that you are of *vata* constitution.

ROLE OF CONSTITUTION IN HEALTH PROGRAMMES

Vata constitution persons will be interested in dry, cold, bitter, pungent and astringent tastes. Irregular food intake aggravates *vata* gets accentuated in persons who are exposed to cold. To control and to cure *vata*, it is better to take hot, sweet, sour and salty food. Certain activities must also be restricted or stopped for pacifying *vata*.

In *pitta* constitution individuals are in the habit of taking pungent, sour, and salty food. This kind of diet aggravates *pitta* and such people are more irritable and prone to hypertension. *Pitta* increases at noon and midnight. It is safer for *pitta* persons to stop eating pungent, sour and salty foods and exposing themselves to hot climate.

Those with *kapha* constitution like to take oily, dull, heavy food and eat more of sweets. Sitting idle lead to aggravation of *kapha* and produces diabetes, obesity and arteriosclerosis. *Kapha* will be more in the morning (6-10 a.m.) and after meals.

The knowledge of constitution is useful for preventing the disease. Ayurveda has given a vivid description of the different constitutions with relevance to maintenance of body and mental health.

The constitution may be changed by adopting *Japa*, *Tapa*, penance, chanting of mantras and meditation, especially transcendental meditation. Practising this changes the mind, which in turn brings about metabolic and physiological changes in the body.

A balanced constitution is always safer, otherwise only one *prakriti* person will always suffer from many diseases. For example, *vata* constitution individuals will suffer from more nervous diseases. The life will be full of agony and unhappiness will creep in.

MARRIAGE COUNCIL

Those with a *pitta* constitution must not get married to one another. Such a marriage must be avoided in the interest of smooth and healthy life. The *kapha* constitution people can well manage with *pitta* or *kapha*.

VATA CONSTITUTION

Section 'A': Interrogatory Examination

Way of your activities	very quickly
Whether you will be excited	very quickly
Power of receptive to new things	fast
Mode of your memory	short
Capacity of hunger, digestion	irregular
Quantity of food you consume	sometime more, sometime less
Which taste you prefer	sweet, sour, salty
Nature of Thirst	minimum
What type of food prefer—cold or hot	warm food
Which type of drinks hot—cold	hot
Whether your bowels move regularly	irregular
What about your constipation	hard constipated stools
Whatkind of sweat you get	more with offensive smell

What about sexual instinct	less
How many issues	small family, 1 or 2
Are you getting good sleep	less with disturbance, 5-6 hrs.
Whether you dream daily	flying, flights, jumping, running, fearfulness
Nature of talking problems	with worries with unsuitable mind, with no self-control
Nature of talk	very fast but with missing of words
Nature of walk	very fast with fast movements
Nature of movements of legs, hands, eyebrows, during your duties or work.	simultaneously, yes

VATA CONSTITUTION

Section 'B': Physical Examination

Face as seen in a mirror	non specific
Chest visible ribs	short, long ribs not seen
Abdomen	thin
Eyes colour	protruded-small, rough eyelashes, thin, dilated pupils
Eye conjunctiva colours	blue or blackish
Tongue	darkish
Teeth	larger or small,

	cracked, protruded, irregular and rough inconsistency
Lips	dry blackish
Body frame	lean/short or long
Weight of body	light, 2-20 lbs less than average
Body strength	weak
Tendency of body	rough, dry, emaciated, lean
Body hairs	scanty
Body smell	none or offensive
Notice your legs, hands, eyebrows and neck	always with movements but quick and light in nature
Skin complexion	bluish or dark black
Skin consistency	cracking, rough, portwine marks
Skin moistness	dry
Temperatures of the skin	low, cold, feet and hands, cold chest
Joints	loose, rigid, cracking with unsteadiness
Tendons	unsteady, cracking with rigidness
Footprints	not defined
Nails	dry, rough, tough, short grows slowly

Hands	dry, rough, tough, short, grows slowly, dry but blackish
Rasa-Nutrient: raise the leg up to 90° C and watch the emptying and filling up time after lowering to normal	more
Pulse	irregularly regular, speedy left on index finger
Eyes	opened during sleep

PITTA CONSTITUTION

Section 'A' Interrogatory Examination

Way of your activities	medium
Whether you will be excited	medium
Power of receptive to new things	quick
Mode of your memory	medium
Capacity of hunger, digestion	good
Quantity of food you consume	more
Which taste you prefer	sweet, bitter, astringent
Nature of thirst	more
Prefer food cold or hot	cold
Which type of drinks hot/cold	cold
Whether your bowels move regularly	twice a day
What about your constipation	loose stools
Do you ever sweat	very easily
What about your sexual instinct	medium
How many issues	medium, 2 or 4
Are you getting good sleep	less but good
Whether you dream daily	violence occasionally,

Nature of talking problems	lightening, fiery angry, with irritation
Nature of talk	fast and clear ideas
Nature of walk	medium with pressure on the ground movement
Nature of movements of legs, hands, eyebrows during your duties of work.	simultaneously yes

PITTA CONSTITUTION

Section 'B': Physical Examination

Face as seen in a mirror	white reddish delicate, one in 100 people
Chest visible ribs	medium but with fat
Abdomen	medium
Eyes colour	penetrating sharp eyelashes brown copper white
Eye conjunctiva colours	yellow reddish
Tongue	coppery
Teeth	moderate but yellow
Lips	copper colour
Body frame	medium
Weight of body	medium normal
Body strength	stronger, moderate
Tendency of body	soft
Body hairs	copper colour

Body smell	foetid smell in armpits
Body movements, notice your legs, hands, eyebrows and neck	precise and sharp
Skin complexion	fairly good and reddish
Skin consistency	smooth, moles and freckles
Skin moistness	slightly oily
Temperatures of the skin	low and sometimes hot forehead
Joints	flabby
Tendons	—
Footprints	not defined
Nails	less oily with copper colour
Hands	moist coppery colour
Rasa-Nutrient: raise the leg up to 90° C and watch the emptying and filling up time after lowering to normal pulse	minimum hot sharp, full volume on middle finger
Eyes	reddish due to hot bath, sun and anger

KAPHA CONSTITUTION

Section A: Interrogatory Examination

Way of your activities	slow
Whether you will be exited	slow
Power of receptive to new things	slow
Mode of your memory	long
Capacity of digestion	slow

How much quantity of food you consume	less
Which taste you prefer	pungent, bitter, astringent
Nature of thirst	minimum
What type of food you prefer	dry and warm
Which type of drinks	hot
Whether your bowls move regularly	once, regular
What about your constipation	well formed stools
Do you ever sweat	less
What about your sexual instinct	more
How many issues	large family more than 5
Are you getting good sleep	6 hrs, maximum 8 hrs
Whether you get dreams daily	water lakes, birds, rivers, garlands, swans and clouds
Nature of talking problems	with stable mind, problems solved peacefully with clear mind but slowly and steadily
Nature of talk	slow with clear and interesting way
Nature of walk	slowly but with pressure on the ground
Nature of movements of legs, hands, eyebrows during your duties of work	simultaneously yes

KAPHA CONSTITUTION

Section B: Physical Examination

Face as seen in a mirror	bright, fair looking attractive one in 1000 people
Chest visible ribs	strong and wide
Abdomen	thick, large
Eyes colour	big but attractive filled with milky type
Eye conjunctiva colours	glossy white
Tongue	clear and light
Teeth	white and large strong
Lips	oily
Body frame	large, fleshy, plump and fat body
Weight of body	heavy, 5-20 lbs more than normal
Body strength	quite strong
Tendency of body	glossy but soft
Body hairs	plenty but very thick and dark
Body smell	no smell
Notice your legs, hands, eyebrows and neck	slow and very slow
Skin complexion	whitish in colour
Skin consistency	soft and clear, cold, glossy
Skin moistness	oily or unctuous
Temperature of the skin	low
Joints	strong, firm, well knit and compact

Tendons	----
Footprints	well defined
Nails	soft, glossy, white, smooth, long, well grown but thick in consistency
Hands	oily or unctuous.
Rasanutrient: raise the leg up to 90°C and watch the emptying and filling up time after lowering to normal pulse	less slow but heavy, felt on ring finger (forefinger)
Eyes	happiness, large attractive with thick eyebrows.

Chapter Three

THE THREE DOSHAS: REAL MAKERS OF MIND AND BODY

An Ayurvedic doctor sees the signs and symptoms of three *doshas* in a patient. The *doshas* are not at all visible. So, only their signs can be gazed for diagnosing diseases. These *doshas* are movable from one place to another and sometimes get obstructed and occluded. They sometimes increase or decrease. They cannot be assessed according to modern medicinal angle.

HOW TO SEE THE DOSHAS

In your body if you want to visualise the heart, kidneys, liver and blood, then one has to see the signs of *tridoshas*. Very rarely, you require radiogram and scanning of the body. Just like adjusting TV for the required programmes, one has to adjust the body either by increase or decrease of the *doshas* through the change of food, climate and changes in the activities of the person.

You can see the *doshas* if a person loses temper out of bounds for *pitta*, and worrying too much with sleeplessness for *vata*. The increase in weight of the person, with heaviness and robustness is seen in case of *kapha*. The *vata* will digest food quickly and always will be lean. The person will have indigestion, coldness in the body, less intake of food, as can be seen in *kapha*. There will be excessive heat, excessive digestion, as he eats too much without satisfaction seen in *pitta*. The entire activities, movement of the body, circulation of the body, and in the tissues and cells controlled by *vata* can be compared to nervous system.

The digestive fire and enzymes digestion, assimilation endocrine secretions are all due to *pitta*. The coldness in the body, cough and asthma are all due to *kapha*.

THE PLACE OF DOSHAS

The *doshas* have proper places and also the main place and their substations. To quote an example, the *vata* is mainly located in the large gut. But all the five sub *doshas* are located in five sub stations. *Apanavayu* is situated below the umbilicus and carries out the expulsion of the foetus, faeces and urine. The *samana vayu* is situated in the lower part of stomach and upper part of the small intestine. It is located near the digestive fire, and moves all over the alimentary tract. It helps in consuming food digestion and assimilation of food and differentiation of food into nutrient and excreta.

Imbalance of *apanavata*—diarrhoea, constipation, colitis, abdomen pain, menses troubles and enlarged prostate are produced due to imbalance of *vata*.

Vyana Vayu is located in the heart and it regulates the circulation of the entire body and movement and activities of the body through the nervous system. Imbalance of it causes hemiplegia, praplegia and ptosis of eyelids and so on.

The *pranavata* is situated in the brain and it controls all the movements of the body including closing and opening of eyelids.

Imbalance of *pranavata* leads to hypertension, improper circulation, irregular heart beat and stress etc. When a person has anxiety, worry, insomnia, overactive mind, cough, hiccups, asthma, pleurisy and respiratory problems, then it is due to *pranavayu* aggravation or imbalance.

Udanavata is located in the throat and lungs and in the umbilicus. This physically controls the speech and the strength of the person and colour of the body. Its imbalance causes speech defects, dry coughs, tonsillitis, ear ache and fatigue.

The *pitta-sub doshas* are responsible mainly for digestion and metabolism. The pitta is nothing but digestive fire. The heat of the body is also controlled by it. There are five sub-*pittas*—*pachaka pitta, ranjaka pitta, sadhaka pitta, alochaka pitta* and *bhrajaka pitta*. The proper vision and sharp thinking are also *pitta* functions.

Pachaka pitta is located in the stomach and small intestine. The main seat of *pitta* is in the small gut. The sub-*dosha* of it is *pachaka pitta* which is mainly responsible for digestion. The smallest, atomic types of cells receive the nutrient through the digestion and it differentiates food into nutrients and waste products. The efficiency of digestion is also controlled by it, by making it hot, slow, or more or less.

Imbalance of *pachaka pitta* leads to acid eructation, burning sensation in the oesophagus, gastric or duodenal ulcer or peptic ulcer, due to excessive *pachaka pitta*.

Ranjaka pitta is located in spleen, liver and red blood cells of the body. This sub *dosha* is responsible for the production of red blood corpuscles, control of blood chemistry and supply of nutrients to the organs through the circulation are all controlled and regulated by it.

Imbalance of *ranjaka pitta* is due to improper and polluted air, water and food, alcohol, smoking of cigarettes and lethargy. When *ranjaka pitta* is imbalanced, it produces thirst, insomia, hunger, jaundice, anaemia, skin and blood diseases.

Sadhaka pitta is located in the heart. It controls the memory and contentment of the person. The *dharma, artha, kama* and *moksha* are being controlled by it, as the heart is the main place for securing all these. The intellect, memory and the retention are all controlled by the *sadhaka pitta*. If any one is defective in a person, then, one must conclude that *sadhaka pitta's* functions are at stake.

Imbalance of *sadhaka pitta* causes heart diseases. Anginapectoris (heart pain), loss of memory, loss of intellect and anger, sadness and defects in taking proper decisions are all due to it.

Alochaka pitta is situated in the eyes. One's sight depends on *alochaka pitta*. When it is in balance, it gives clear healthy and bright eyes. When a person is aggravated and excited, you can see the redness in the eyes. Excessive alcohol intake also produces the same effect. A hot head bath also produces the same effect. It is due to imbalance of *alochaka pitta*.

Imbalance of *alochaka pitta* produces all sorts of eye troubles—defective vision, blindness and cataract.

Bhrajaka pitta is a sub *dosha* of *pitta* and it is located in the skin. When it is in balanced state, the skin will be shiny leading to happiness.

Imbalance of *bhrajaka pitta* produces reddish inflammed skin. Skin diseases such as skin cancer, boils, scabies and red rashes are all very common.

KAPHA

Kapha has five sub *doshas* and there are a total of sixteen sub *doshas* viz. *kledaka kapha, avalambhaka kapha, bhodaka kapha, tarpaka kapha* and lastly *sleshaka kapha*. When the *kapha* is in a balanced state, it lubricates the cells, tissues and organs and also it binds them together. The taste, smell, and moist sense are all controlled by it.

Kledaka kapha is located in the stomach. This is necessary for digestion for making food properly lubricated. It is present in the lining of the stomach (mucus membrane). When *kledaka kapha* is balanced, it produces good lubrication, strong and effective stomach lining and good digestion and assimilation.

Imbalance of *kledaka kapha* produces defective digestion. It may be hyper or hypo type of digestion.

Avalambaka kapha is situated in the heart, chest and lower back. *Kapha's* main seat is in the chest. The person will have a very good chest and shoulders. When balanced, it produces strong muscles of the chest and also it protects the heart muscles.

Imbalance of *avalambaka kapha* produces wheezing, asthma, congestive cardiac failure, congest in the lungs, cold, cough, sluggishness and back pain. All the respiratory diseases are going to be produced due to its imbalance.

Bhodhaka kapha is located in the tongue of the person. This *kapha* is responsible for identifying the tastes of the foods. Fine tasting food leads to good nutrition and growth of the body.

Imbalance of *bhodhaka kapha* leads to allergies, obesity, lethargy, diabetes and congestion in mucus membranes. It leads to impairment of salivary glands and taste buds with loss of taste and indigestion.

Tarpaka kapha's main place is in the head, sinus cavities and cerebrospinal fluids (C.S.F). It nourishes the senses-motor and sensory. Even the eyes are being nourished by it. It nourishes the intellect and memory through cerebrospinal fluid.

Imbalance of *tarpaka kapha*, produces sinusitis. It is very common during its imbalance. Headache of sinusitis, defective in the sense of smell and impairment of other sense organs are also observed.

Sleshaka kapha is situated in the joints of the body. It lubricates the easy movements in the joints. It is necessary for the joints as they are having continuous movements.

Imbalance of *sleshaka kapha* produces almost all joints diseases, arthritis, osteoarthritis and rheumatoid arthritis. When it is imbalanced, the joints will become watery, loose, associated with inflammation—redness, heat, pain and loss of function. Without its presence in the joints, it leads to inflammation and friction pain and later on permanent deformity.

Chapter Four

A PHOTO PRINT OF NATURE

I magine that the train you have been waiting for does not come on time. Some people get anxious and impatient. This is due to *vata* aggravation. Other people start scolding the railway authorities for their imcompetence and become very angry. It is due to *pitta* aggravation. Some simply sit quietly without any comments. This is due to *kapha*.

These elements are included in Ayurveda in body types. *Vata* person becomes restless, *pitta* person has a rash behaviour, *kapha* person is a little dull, and lethargic. In Ayurveda this is called *prakriti*, which is a Sanskrit word meaning constitution.

ONE MUST RESPECT HIS BODY TYPE

One must respect one's *prakriti* in order to live happily and healthily.

Mr. Ramakrishna, a worker, in a hot furnace came to me with skin blisters. He was aggressive, irritable and jealous. His memory was sharp and his dreams full of violence. He had a sharp tongue. His financial status was moderate, but his spending was luxurious.

He was diagnosed as having *pitta* type of *prakriti*. He was asked to leave his present job in favour of a better one. It may be noted here that he used to be happy in cold climate, liked cold drinks and cold food. So, he was advised to change his work place, to have cold food, cold drinks, and to live in calm and cold atmosphere. This is intended to make one's *doshas* happy and to get good health. Here no medicine is prescribed.

ONE WITH NATURE

The man is made up of a particular constitution, which cannot be altered or changed. It can only be balanced. The *vata* will be more after taking dry, rough, cold, pungent, bitter and astringent foods. If a person with *pitta* constitution takes pungent, sour, salty food, in a hot climate, he will feel unhealthy. The *kapha* personality will be subjected to change in his attitude due to exposing to cold food, cold climate and laziness with excessive intake of sweets. In a man, all the three *doshas* are there and one will be predominant. So, one must live with them. The *doshas* will have the psychological symptoms which are dealt here.

Vata

Sensitive, imaginative, good memory, fearful and insecure.

Pitta

Aggressive, irritable, jealous, confident, joyous, intellectual and sharp in memory.

Kapha

Courageous, prolonged memory, emotionally calm, greedy, loving, sympathetic, courageous and bold.

When these are found in a person, we can conclude that he is in perfect health, due to perfect balance of *doshas*.

Everyone wants to be slim and healthy especially women. They go to gymnasium or sports club for trimming their body. But, this is more or less a muscle exercise rather than a change. Ayurveda persons with *vata* are lean, thin and charming. A *pitta* person is medium in build, has self-control and is easily attracted by others. A *kapha* person has a solid body, is short in stature and more proned to diabetes. *Vata* persons are more prone to nervous disorder. *Pitta* persons are liable to bilious and digestive disorders.

The *doshas* cannot be changed, as they are from birth. They can only be balanced. The increased *dosha* can be decreased and decreased *dosha* can be increased. When the *doshas* are disturbed and imbalanced, they will have the following physical symptoms and signs:

When Vata is imbalanced

1. Spasm in the body or contraction
2. Pains or aches in the body
   Myalgia—muscle pain; neuralgia—nerve pain
   arthralgia—joints pain
3. Cramps—muscle cramps—after exercise or sports or after too much sexual act
4. Nervousness—One will shake his body when *vata* is imbalanced, eg Parkinsonism
5. Distension of abdomen
6. Emaciation
7. Constipation

When Pitta is imbalanced

1. Fever
2. More hungry-more eating
3. Excessive thirst
4. Heart burn or gastritis
5. Red skin or rashes
6. Inflammation

When Kapha is imbalanced

1. Excessive sleep
2. Heaviness in the body
3. Cold, cough
4. Rhinitis, running nose
5. Mucous discharge
6. Congestion in nose

7. Congestion in lungs
8. Congestion in sinus
9. Swelling in the body—due to fluid retention
10. Less digestive fire
11. Lethargy
12. No interest to do anything
13. Diabetes

People with *vata dosha* are frequently constipated. This may be due to even with other two *doshas*.

When these *doshas* are vitiated, then, he will have mental and physical disorders.

Symptoms are the complaints of the patient and the science elicited by the doctor on examination of the patient.

Vata types of person

1. Chronic constipation
2. Anxiety and neurosis
3. Depression
4. Pains—chronic in nature
5. Cramps in muscles
6. Hypertension
7. Irritable colon syndrome
8. Menopausal syndrome
9. Dysmenorrhoea
10. Premenstrual tension

Pitta type of persons

Are more susceptible to:

1. Ulcers—peptic, gastric, duodenal
2. Skin rashes
3. Poor eye sight due to less vitamin A
4. Heart burn—due to acidity
5. Hair fall—baldness
6. Heart attacks-due to stress and strain
7. Self-criticism

Kapha types of persons

Are more prone to:

1. Cold
2. Diabetes
3. Obesity
4. Arthritis—rheumatoid
5. Asthma-bronchial
6. Allergic—cough-asthma
7. High cholesterol
8. Congestion in chest, sinus
9. Indigestion, loss of appetite
10. Heaviness in the body
11. Excessive sleep
12. Lethargy

The above symptoms are present in a person with different *doshas*. It does not give any guarantee not to occur together or clubbed with other symptoms.

The cold, tamaka swasa (bronchial asthma) are due to first *vata* and later *kapha*. The seat of these to occur is in stomach and not in the lungs as advocated in western medicine. When a person is anxious and irritable, it is due to *vata* first and later *pitta dosha*.

Imbalance of body

Is due to imbalance in the mind.

The symptoms of a balanced mind are:

1. Clear
2. Happy
3. Sensitive
4. Alert
5. Bravery
6. Contentment
7. Simplicity
8. Calmness

9. Faith in God
10. Humility
11. Quickness

When the mind is imbalanced these factors will be either absent or disturbed.

DISEASE AND ITS SUBTLENESS

Mrs. Sumitha underwent an operation of the uterus. It was removed due to excessive bleeding (menorrhagia). She complained of pain in the body. She took medicines from western doctors, but got no relief. She came to me for consultation. She complained that she had not slept after the operation. Analgesics—pain relievers did not work. I explained to her that in any injury or operation, the *vata* will be aggravated and hence the pain. This is due to the imbalance of body and mind due to *vata dosha*.

She was put on balancing *vata* schedule-meditation, *vata* pacifying diet, and rest. She was relieved of her pain and insomnia. To quote another example for *pitta* provocation.

Mr. Smith, a journalist, was in the habit of drinking coffee 10-12 times in a day, taking less food, that too, at irregular intervals and also he was under stress due to his work.

He developed gastric ulcer and was advised an operation. Gastro-Jejunostomy linking stomach with Jejunum, was done. He came to me for consultation and was put on rest, milk diet and *pitta* alleviating diet. He was asked to refrain from irregular eating habits, coffee and alcohol. He was asked to take physical and mental rest to get his *doshas* balanced.

SYMPTOMS OF IMBALANCE OF PITTA

1. Anger
2. Tension

3. Hyper acidity in the body
4. More gastric juice—gastritis
5. Inflammed digestive canal
6. Burning sensation in the body
7. Burning in the head
8. Burning in the foot and palms

The ulcer production depends mainly on provocation of *pitta*. This is so in the majority of cases. The ulcer can be pacified and cured with *pitta* pacifying diet, rest, and meditation. The details of *pitta* pacifying diet are explained in part 'B' and part 'C'. Tuberculosis and cancer are produced due to imbalanced state of *tridoshas* and not with one *dosha*. Tuberculosis of the lungs is due to excess *kapha dosha*.

REASON FOR IMBALANCE OF DOSHAS

The doshas get imbalanced due to diet and activities and changes in the external atmosphere. The powerful *dosha* that first goes into vitiation is *vata*. If *vata* is aggravated, then, it triggers and imbalances the entire *pitta* and *kapha*.

IMBALANCE OF VATA

By nature, a *vata* person is always cheerful and full of enthusiasm. This is a balanced state. From childhood to old age, people suffer from different types of aches or pains. Higher class of people suffer from *vata* imbalance. They will take sleeping pills, analgesics and tranquilisers. These are going to produce adverse reactions in the body and changes in the mind.

The majority of diseases are due to *vata* imbalance, backache, premenstrual pain and depression disappear as soon as the *vata* is brought into balance. *Vata* occurs more in old age. The skin shrinks, muscles become flabby and a person gets fatigued quickly. Life becomes miserable. These are not produced due to normal *vata*, but due to its imbalance. Paralysis, hemiplegia and ciatica are all due to its imbalance.

Vata controls all the functions of the body which includes the nervous system. Mental symptoms such as grief shock, anxiety, fear, fatigue and exhaustion are all due to it. It works like electricity in the body.

WHY IT HAPPENS

In a *vata prakriti* person, there is likelihood of vata imbalance. One must look out for the following symptoms:

1. Emotional-grief, shock, fear
2. Dry-weather and cold atmosphere
3. On empty stomach and fasting
4. Irregular drinks
5. Irregular food
6. Untimely food
7. Cold-food, dry, pungent bitter and astringent
8. Sleepless nights
9. Anxiety and stress due to overwork
10. Physical exertion
11. Addiction to alcohol, smoking
12. Sudden change of place with change in diet

An Ayurvedic physician will diagnose the *vata*—imbalance with the following signs and symptoms.

PHYSICAL COMPLAINTS

1. Dry skin
2. Fatigue
3. Gas trouble
4. Distension of abdomen
5. Susceptible cold
6. Pains of different nature
7. Loss of weight
8. Muscle pains-cramps
9. Nervous aches

10. Low back pain
11. Premenstrual pain
12. Irritable colon syndrome
13. Hypertension
14. Cracked lips
15. Cracked skin
16. Highly talkative

BEHAVIOURAL PROBLEMS

1. Restlessness
2. Loss of appetite
3. Loss of sleep
4. Weakness
5. No mood to relax

MENTAL PROBLEMS

1. Psychosis
2. Depression
3. Anxiety
4. Worry
5. No patience
6. Loss of concentration

These symptoms are due to *vata* imbalance. They may also be produced due to imbalance of other two *doshas*. Sometimes they simulate or mimic these symptoms.

IMBALANCE OF PITTA

When pitta is in balance, the person is sweet natured, always joyous and enthusiastic and a good body build. *pitta* is nothing but digestive fire. So he eats and grows well. When a young girl develops pimples on her face, one thinks it is due to *pitta* imbalance. The hair starts falling. Baldness starts at the age of forty or even earlier. Because of good appetite and digestion, the body grows out of proportion leading to gastric ulcers, heart burn and heart problems. These are all due to stress and strain. This has been established in research on animals like rabbits. The vata also goes into imbalance and gets mixed up with pitta and creates more problems such as hypertension, hemiplegia, paraplegia, facial paralysis and ciatica.

WHY IT HAPPENS

When pitta is balanced in a person, the behaviour will be smooth. Overwork will imbalance the *pitta*. When the *pitta* is imbalanced one must look for the following symptoms:

1. Exposed to hot sun
2. Exposed to hot furnace
3. Exposed to hot climate
4. Exposed to stress and strain
5. Eating hot, pungent chillies and other spicy foods
6. Use of more salt
7. Use of fermented foods
8. Use of sour foods
9. Over ambitious in nature

PHYSICAL COMPLAINTS

1. Ulcers
2. Acidity-hyperacidity
3. Sour body smell
4. Haemorrhoids
5. Skin boils, rashes and acne
6. Offensive breath
7. Excessive appetite
8. Excessive thirst
9. Sunstroke
10. Heat stroke
11. Red hot eyes

BEHAVIOURAL PROBLEMS

Loss of temper, critical of always others and is prone to arguments.

MENTAL CONDITIONS

Irritability with depression, anger, self criticism and impatience and restlessness.

Any *dosha* imbalance may produce any symptoms, but these are the common signs and symptoms of *pitta* imbalance.

IMBALANCE OF KAPHA

Kapha is required for growth of the body and mind. It can be anabolic steroids of modern medicine. It is more in young age and at morning time.

When the Kapha is in balance, then a person becomes calm, quiet, affectionate and forgiving. He is strong and steady in body and mind.

When the *kapha* is imbalanced one can notice frequent cold, cough and sinus. The person often feels sleepy, is lazy, eats too much and grows fat, leading to arteriosclerosis, diabetes and high blood pressure. When the *kapha* gets imbalanced too much, he is rejected by people and dejected by himself and has difficulty in breathing, swelling all over the body and lastly, he suffers from congestive cardiac failure. They withstand problems, so they rarely go to doctors.

Kapha is more imbalanced due to intake of excess of sweets. Milk and its products aggravate the *kapha*. The imbalance of *kapha* produces sinus and lung complaints, headache due to sinusitis, hayfever, bronchial asthma and congestion in the chest and in some people food allergy. Some people are allergic to non-vegetarian diet and some are allergic even to milk or to cold climate. This differs from individual to individual.

WHEN IT HAPPENS

When you suffer from influenza or cold, allergies, cough, bronchial asthma and later obesity, the following are going to influence them one way or the other either as a causative factor or as aggravating agents:

1. He is in the habit of having more and more things and store them
2. Cold weather
3. Damp climate, excess snowfall
4. He depends on others for everything
5. Sleeping too much
6. Lethargic

An Ayurveda physician will try to diagnose *kapha* imbalance with the following signs and symptoms.

PHYSICAL PROBLEMS

1. High cholesterol
2. High lipids
3. Frequent colds
4. Weight gain
5. Cold, allergy, bronchial asthma
6. Cough with expectoration
7. Diabetes
8. Susceptibility to cold and cold weather
9. Sinusitis-sinus inflammation
10. Swelling of the body-due to excess fluids retention
11. Pallor of skin
12. Arthritis-rheumatoid
13. Pneumonia-chest congestion
14. Tuberculosis of the lungs
15. Heaviness in the body

Chapter Five

RESTORING BALANCE

—Common Views

Ayurveda's main intension is to bring back a balanced state of mind and body to promote perfect health.

Mr. Satya, a businessman of 35 years, was suffering from sleeplessness for the last ten years. He was overactive lean and thin. He was quick in taking decisions, was sensitive and imaginative in nature. So I diagnosed him of *vata parkriti*. He used to remain awake at night. He used to kill time by reading periodicals and newspapers and was irregular in taking food and was an alcoholic. I advised him to go to bed before 10 p.m. and stop drinking and to take oil bath daily for a week. On the very first day of the oil bath he got sleep. The use of vata alleviating diet and exercise made him to get the *doshas* to a balanced state.

A MULTI CHANNEL THERMOSTATS

Our body consists of a nervous system, which is full of sensitive thermostats. Our blood supplies proper nutrients to muscles, liver, spleen, and kidney. Carbohydrates, fat, and proteins are supplied to organs without fail through the circulation of blood.

The entire process of the body is controlled by mind, which is situated in hypothalamus. It is only one-sixth of an ounce. It regulates and controls the following functions: Appetite, sleeping, awakening, digestion, fat, carbohydrate metabolism, thirst, body temperature, growth of the body. All these things are going on inside our body without our notice or control. So all these things depend on the brain. The brain keeps the balanced state. Hence the mind must be kept under control with suitable meditation, *japa, tapa* and balanced breathing. Nature understands and it makes us to understand and it guides us to change the diversities to normal state.

A *vata prakriti* person will be aggravated with the following things:

Pungent and spicy foods, sleeping late at night, cold food, cold climate, dry foods and fear, eating very little at odd hours. Prakriti of a person will go into a stage of *vikriti* which is opposed to nature. Taking food at odd hours or not at all taking food is unnatural. Not sleeping at a proper time is also against nature. One must go to sleep before 10 p.m. After 10 p.m. *pitta* time starts and so one *does* not get sleep.

All these things make the body and mind imbalanced. With all these irregularities a person will become impatient. He will lose confidence in himself and suffer from permanent sleeplessness and loss of memory.

A *vata prakriti* person does not want to move with too many people and hear loud noises. The modern stress and strain of living will accentuate the imbalance further. In the initial stages, the body tries to reject and bring the imbalanced state to balanced state of mind and body. In order to set *vata* to balanced state, it is necessary that a person should be calm, sleep at the right times, take food at time and in proper quantity. This is natural or *prakriti*.

VIKRITI (PATHOLOGICAL)

Vata prakriti dosha is easily disturbed and aggravated and it disturbs *pitta* and *kapha*.

Mr. Sathya was able to understand the sequence of changes taking place within him and all efforts were made to bring back *vata* to its normal and original status. This is the efficacy of Ayurveda.

Later Mr. Sathya was taught the new routines in order to soothe his perturbed *doshas*. A list of pacifying *doshas* was given to him. First thing to be followed was his daily habits of sleeping at 10 p.m. and taking evening food at 8 p.m. and meditation at 6 a.m. and 6 p.m.

He was asked to take an oil bath before going to bed. The oil used was sesame oil. He was advised to take 1 cup of buffalo milk with one teaspoonful of chyavanprasha or aswagandha leha (Lehya-Linctus). He was allowed to hear music before sleeping, to promote soundness and coolness in the brain.

He followed this routine feeling and got good sleep and woke up in the morning, fresh and active.

SIX STAGES OF DISEASE PROCESS

The main aim of Ayurveda medicine is to bring him back from imbalanced state to balance.

Whenever a person is removed from a job or suffers mental shock due to the death of a close person, the entire immune system becomes upset and leads to unnecessary physical and mental defects.

In Ayurveda, the process of disease formation takes place in six different stages. The first three stages are not at all visible to us, but the last three stages are noticeable in terms of symptoms. So in every stage, the balance of the system is at bay or lost.

The six stages of disease process are explained as under:

1. **Accumulation: (Sanchaya)**
   This occurs with building up of either one or more *dosha* or more.

2. **Aggravation: (Prakopa)**
   This accumulated excess *dosha* enters the place and starts spreading from its nearest boundaries.

3. **Dissemination: (Prasara)**
   The accumulated and aggravated *dosha* starts spreading all over the body.
4. **Localisation: (Stana Samsraya)**
   The above *doshas* start settling down to a particular place.

5. **Manifestation: (Vyakiti)**

   The symptoms of the *doshas* will occur physically at the place of localisation.
6. **Disruption: (Bheda)**
   Now it is a state, where in you find all the symptoms and signs of the disease.

Let us think that *kapha* is accumulated in the *kapha* body type of a person. As soon as the excess *kapha* is accumulated it starts moving around the body, bidding good bye to its original spot or place and gets blocked. This is called Ama (undigested material or toxic residue). This stage completes, the third stage of the disease processes. A western doctor cannot diagnose as present texts do not give an explanation of this stage of the disease. Ayurveda says that this is the fourth stage and the patient is not perfectly healthy. One can sense the *kapha dosha* imbalance as there is pain all over the body, mild temperature and fatigue. The patient becomes sick. Indigestion, excess salivation, heaviness, and loss of sleep seen in the patient. It is very easy to treat at the first, second and third stages with suitable herbs, diet, daily routine, exercise and if necessary purificatory methods as *pancha karma* therapy. This is explained in the forth-coming chapters of part 'B'. After the diseases are fully developed, it needs immediate attention of an Ayurvedic doctor, as the above solution is not suitable.

In the fourth stage, vague pains occurring very frequently due to dietary indiscretion, behavioural and emotional upsets cause imbalances of *doshas*, which will be lodged and it needs purification of *dosha*. The *vata*, *pitta* and *kapha* are brought into a state of natural balance. The fundamental approach of attending to *doshas* with small changes in food, daily routine, herbs, exercises bring dynamic results. This also holds good in serious case of diseases.

WAY TO BALANCING DOSHAS

The details given here are meant only for preventing the diseases and not for curing them. It is always safer and better to consult an Ayurveda doctor, who will be able to give you a detailed medical routine for the specific ailment.

IMPORTANT TIPS FOR BALANCING LIFE

For balancing vata:

1. Massaging with til oil (sesame)
2. Good nourishing diet
3. Warmth for body
4. Sufficient rest to body
5. Avoid stress and strain
6. Calm and quiet
7. Regulate your habits

Vata is the king of *doshas*. It is supreme commander. It regulates and controls the movements of *pitta* and *kapha*. By correcting and balancing the *vata*, you can hit at it and get the benefit for two. *Vata* can be compared to wind in the external atmosphere, which moves clouds from one place to another slowly or rapidly. So also in the body, *vata* activates and triggers the movements of pitta and *kapha*. It is like a main board switch. As soon as it is switched on, the whole body activities are triggered and made to work. This is required not only for circulation of blood and respiration, but also for the cells at quantum level of mind and body.

So it is better to cultivate good habits in a balanced way.

1. The balanced way for *vata* is massage with sesame oil
2. Hot water bath to body and lukewarm water to head
3. Rest, physical and mental
4. Sleep before 10 p.m. (go to bed at night)
5. Meditation 6 a.m. to 6 p.m. 5-10 minutes (Transcendental). The Maharshi International have developed transcendental meditation. It is good to practice
6. Warm: Keep your body warm. It is good for *vata* as its property is cold, do not expose to cold air and take cold food
7. Eat *vata* pacifying diet (part C)

It is good to take food regularly and in time and when it is warm, schedule is two meals with a breakfast. It is better to take dry or wet ginger before lunch and shatapushpa (somph) after meals, which stimulates digestion.

HOT OR WARM DRINKS

Drink only warm fluids as they are good for *vata* and have qualities quite opposed to *vata*.

1. Avoid stress and strain
2. Avoid loud noise or music
3. Keep your place with good illumination and clean and tidy
4. Sunlight is good, so keep the doors and windows open

For *vata* sunlight is good. Do not go outside for long time. Keep yourself engaged with cheerful and humorous reading material.

Good–bye to drinks

It is better to bid good bye to drinks, alcohol, tea, coffee and smoking cigarettes. Avoid worries and tension.

NASAL DROPS (NASYA)

For all the diseases of the head, neck, eye, ear, and nose, *nasya* is the best treatment. In cold climate, the nose gets dry, hence you have to put 5 drops of sesame oil into it. Then do mild massage to the nose. This is not to be done in sinusitis as there is already blockage. The oil precipitates *kapha* and there will be excess pain and headache. The errhine therapy can be repeated 3 to 4 times or more in a day, for non-sinus trouble patients. This is useful for all types of people. It tones up the sinuses and keeps the mind tranquil.

HOW TO BALANCE PITTA

All things for the mind and body must be in moderation. Pitta balancing is done with cold food, cold air and cold atmosphere. *Pitta dosha* persons are quite aggressive and hot in behaviour. Pungent, sour and salt will imbalance *pitta dosha*. Alcoholic drinks also do the same. One is very angry and forcible in nature. They are quarrelsome and highly emotional in their behaviour. The following points will keep the *pitta* in a balanced state.

REST

Rest plays a very important role here. It must be for both mind and body. It controls your emotions, anxiety, and tension.

1. Eat calm lunch, take rest and avoid disturbances of any kind.
2. Meditation is the best source for keeping the mind in tranquility and peace and prevent any further aggressiveness.

3. One should not take heavy meals.
4. Cold things will balance the *pitta*. Cold bath is good
5. When *pitta* is vitiated cold and sweet fruit drinks are recommended. Dry grapes, grapes and apple juice are good.
6. Drink plenty of fluids.
7. Stay in a place surrounded by water.
8. Very cold foods are contraindicated, as they pacify the digestive fire.
9. Eat *pitta* pacifying diet. (Part-C).
10. Don't skip meal as it may produce ulcers.
11. If digestion is high, then drink milk with sugar candy. It will help to bring back *pitta* into balance. If there is excessive appetite and excessive thirst, it is better to keep them in moderation with *pitta* alleviating diet (Part C).
12. Excessive hunger can be pacified not by reducing diet, but taking bitter vegetables like bitter gourd and bitter beans and bitter green vegetables. These are stated in *Charaka Samhita*, a compendium of medicine, an authority of Ayurveda medicine.
13. Avoid soft drinks as they increase *pitta*. Alcohol is like a petrol to digestive fire, which makes the appetite extraordinarily great and burns the intestines and liver.
14. Bread and fermented foods are also not good for *pitta*.

Laxatives are best for balancing the pitta dosha. The use of castor oil is also good for that purpose. **Caution:** People with ulcer of stomach and intestine disorders are advised not to use it as it may cause damages to intestine and perforation. In case there is loss of water, then it is better to drink warm water. The next day the person feels light and fresh. It is digestive and diuretic. Orange or apple juice is to be taken the next day of *virechana*.

FOOD

Pure food, pure water and fresh air are only good to *pitta* persons. Adulterated food, water and air will promote imbalance of *pitta*. Avoid artificial food additives, as they create metabolic disturbance with imbalance of *pitta*.

TIPS

1. Avoid exposure to hot sun.
2. Avoid exposure to fire.
3. Going out in morning and evening, will balance the *pitta*. Cold lotions like sandal, *sariva chandana* are good to balance *pitta*.
4. Avoid violent pictures, books, controversial TV serials and smoking as these increase *pitta*.
5. **Sounds**: smooth sounds, songs, and music pleasing to the mind and body are advocated. Laughter is the best medicine for *pitta dosha*. Enjoy nature and beauty, as it cools down *pitta*.

HOW TO BALANCE KAPHA

1. Less sweets
2. Warm clothes
3. Warm foods
4. Warm drinks
5. Warm climate
6. Activities
7. Regular exercise controls your weight
8. Regular walking for 2 to 4 kilometres per day

Kapha dosha needs activity, either exercise, walk or tour seeing different people and a variety of places. Otherwise, he will get more sleep and be idle and lethargic. People with *kapha* will have indigestion and less appetite. It may lead on to 'AMA' (undigested toxic material). In order to avoid this, one must engage in work and exercise. Obesity, cold, running nose, allergies and blocked nose are also due to it.

Everything must be warm. Food, clothes, and drinks all these things bring *kapha* to balance, as it is cold dosha in nature.

Honey is the best for *kapha*. Ayurveda has advocated it, although it is sweet. Dry heat is good for nasal congestion or for lungs congestion.

Avoid dampness, cold water, as *kapha* by itself is cold. *Udvartana*, a dry massage is good for the body. The food must be light and easily digested. *Kapha* type of people will get diseased very frequently and get imbalanced soon. Avoid taking *kapha* promoting foods in cold season and winter or else sinusitis will be blown upto the maximum.

HOW TO RECTIFY IMBALANCE OF KAPHA

The following tips will help you to rectify the imbalance of *kapha* and bring it back to balance.

1. **Less sweet**: as otherwise *kapha* will be aggravated and produce heavy weight with diabetes, and high blood pressure.
2. **Eat**: *kapha* pacifying diet (Part C) eat less to avoid over weight. After eating more, use dry ginger or fennel seeds after lunch or dinner, which helps in digestion.
3. **Tastes**: Astringent tastes, dry foods, apples, turmeric powder, raw vegetables, hold good. They decrease *kapha* and tone up digestive fire.
4. **Drinks**: boil coriander and ginger in water and take it with lukewarm as it is good for *kapha*.
5. **Exercises**: good for *kapha* people as it avoids stagnation and creates activity and vigour with strength and stamina.
6. **Avoid**: sedentary habits as sitting idle and sleeping too much.

7. **Congestion**: is frequent and common in the head and nose which can be remedied by inhaling warm salt water through one nostril and leaving in other nostril. Try not to inhale deep, as it may go into lungs and produce diseases.

HOW TO PERFORM UDVARTANA

This is a type of dry massage. This is useful in *kapha* type persons and also in obesity. It promotes circulation and detaches the toxins from the skin of the body.

1. Start massage right from the head to neck in a circular fashion. In the shoulder and wrist, the massage is done from below to upward, circular in shoulder, elbow and wrist joints.
2. In the chest longitudinal or from downward to above is the best massage by avoiding the place of heart.
3. Massage stomach from below upwards 2 to 3 times per day.
4. Proceed to massage the buttock and thigh and their back from below upwards and in hip joint in a circular motion.
5. Massage the legs from below upwards with circular movements in knee and ankle joints and toes.
6. This should be done for 15-20 minutes per day.
7. It is better to use gloves. Preferably use silk gloves or rubber ones for conducting *udvartana*.
8. The massage must not be harsh and uncomfortable.
9. Mahasudharshana *choorna* is used for conducting *udvartana*.

Part B

The Quantum Human Body, Mind and Medicine

Chapter Six

THE QUANTUM HUMAN BODY, MIND AND MEDICINE

Ayurveda is the science of life. It is an embodiment of mind and body. The body and mind are mere a photoprint of nature. The world is composed of five matters—earth, water, fire, air, and ether. These are present in suitable proportions in our body too. *Vata dosha* is formed by space and air and *pitta dosha* is composed of fire and water while *kapha dosha* is the result of water and earth.

Now, we are dealing with quantum human body, which not only shapes the body, but also controls it.

In Part 'A' are stated some fundamental principles that are hidden in the quantum body. All these things are possible through an invisible intelligence. Even a small nail prick will be transmitted to the mind from the physical body through senses, nerves to brain which sends messages to remove the prick of nails. You must know how wonderfully these things are going on in our subtle body.

When a person who is related to youdris, you are shocked and your blood pressure, heart rate and pulse are elevated. This is due to release of adrenaline to the circulation. The mind immediately acts and adrenal gland present in the abdomen starts excessive secretion. So, one can experience all the above signs and symptoms, but cannot see them. It occurs at the quantum level and is more fundamental in nature than matter.

TRY TO DISCOVER THE INNER WORLD

As everybody knows that a matter is solid, stable, touched and measured through weighing. The thoughts of mind are invisible and fluctuating. A man sitting in America can pass his impulses of mind to Bangalore in India. This is quite possible. Doshas are switching stations and if *vata* is less, then, food necessary for *vata* is liked moreby a person. When *vata* is more, then a person dislikes the vata food. This happens in our body not at the atom level but at the quantum level. This is possible only when the mind changes into matter.

Whenever the atmosphere is cold, then the mind must act after in receives the message from the senses. But in case it does not act, then the mind and body link will be disturbed. Strain and stress will be accumulated in the body and mind and as a result, the cells will be damaged resulting in urticaria, allergic signs and symptoms.

QUANTUM MEDICINE

Till now we have discussed the quantum body, but hereafter the quantum medicine for the quantum body will be explained to the readers.

Heart attacks occur but they differ from one individual to other. Mr. Gangadhar works in a factory with his strenuous job is likely not to suffer a heart attack. But a highly placed Mr. Butler, an executive, with less physical exercise is more likely to suffer from heart attack. It can be prevented by taking one orange per day or daily use of garlic or onion in the diet.

This is possible only when a person does not exert his body. Physical body naturally will not have enough strength in terms of nervine and circulatory to withstand any stress and strain of the brain.

To quote another example, thirty-seven-year-old Mr. Rajan Babu, had cancer of the acute promyelocytic leukaemia. Amk-m3 type was treated with chemotherapy at a cost of Rs. seven lakhs and fifty thousand and it was certified that he would live for only two months.

He was treated by an ayurveda doctor, Balenda Prakash, Managing Director, Ayurveda Cancer Research Institute, Dehradun, at only Rs. 1400. After break of a few months, he was given a second course of treatment. He is hale and healthy after years of Ayurveda treatment, and is now working as lecturer in Palakkad Engineering College, Kerala. For details, please read the book *Cancer Therapy in Ayurveda* by this author.

SECOND CASE

Binu was suffering from bilateral Wilm's tumor of kidneys and her life was not guaranteed. Doctor at AIIMS, New Delhi, treated the case and it was monitored by doctors from the US.

She had four operations and a twenty-one course of chemotherapy with no benefits. She was completely cured with Ayurveda treatment and is now attending her routine duties.

These treatments were done without opening the main gates of healing but only with ayurveda medicine. There are several cancer cases rejected by not only Indian, but also cancer specialists of foreign countries.

Ravi, age 16 years, had pseudomuscular hypertrophy and was brought after 3-4 course of western treatment without any benefits. He was reluctant to undergo Ayurveda treatment, as it takes at least one month. However, I convinced him that he will get relief with only one course of *panchakarma* (five actions or therapies). In the first week, he was given oleation therapy with medicated ghee for 7 days and he was subjected to, sudation therapy for another seven days after a break of one week. He was given oil massage along with rock salt. It followed hot water bath to body and lukewarm water to head with medicated water—castor leaves, Nirgundi

(Vitex Nirgundi) leaves and Rasna powder were added to water and boiled for 10-15 minutes.

Then, a course of enema for 16 days alternated with decoction enema and nutritive enema was given. The decoction of *dasamula* (ten drugs) was prepared with honey. Rock salt and sesame oil were added and made warm and administered.

TIME OF ADMINISTRATION

The decoction enema must be give early in the morning before 8 a.m. and it must come out within three-fourths of an hour.

QUANTITY TO BE ADMINISTERED

The official quantity is about one litre, but practically half litre of decoction with honey, *saindhava lavana* (rock salt), paste of drugs and seasame oil are made warm on a water bath and administered. The enema must come out within three-fourths of an hour.

OIL ENEMA

This is simple and must be administered immediately after food. It may not come out soon, as it would not produce any side effect.

QUANTITY

250 ml of oil is usually given. It does not come out soon. It comes out the next day whenever the patient passes motion.

With this, the movement of the body especially his calf muscles and knee joints got a little flexible and he started standing. This case was presented before specialist doctors from twenty countries who came to India on a WHO delegation. They were very pleased with the improvement. They told me that the treatment of pseudomuscular hypertrophy does not respond to western treatments.

He was given another two courses of treatment with suitable *vata* pacifying diet and was discharged. After fifteen years of the treatment, he is hale and healthy and has completed his education and is now, working in Tamil Nadu.

The *panchakarma* procedures detoxify the body and balance the aggravated *doshas*. The internal *vata* pacifying medicine acts at the quantum level and it helps to restore the *doshas* to balance.

THE MENTAL AWARENESS

The patient was made to do meditation in the morning for 15 minutes. It has helped him to have confidence in the treatment. It also balances the mind faculties to derive good health. During the course of treatment, he was given mental rest with suitable diet. This is how quantum medicine works in a quantum human mechanical body to secure perfect health. The ultimate aim and goal of Ayurveda is to promote perfect health to the people.

Chapter Seven

OPENING THE MAIN GATES OF CHANNELS OF HEALING

PANCHAKARMA THERAPY
(Pentad Purificatory Procedures)

The *panchakarma* is a *shodhana* method of treatment. But in Ayurveda, there is a *shamana* treatment of diseases. This is just like symptomatic treatment of modern medicines. The *panchakarma* is pentad of purificatory procedures. The role of *panchakarma* is dislodging and expelling the toxins from each and every cell of the body as soon as the toxins are flushed out of the cells of the body. For example, excess mucus in the chest, bile in the small intestine, *kapha* in the stomach and gas accumulation in the large gut will be eliminated. *Panchakarma* not only cleanses the body but also the mind. The basic five processes are *Vaman* (emesis), *Virechana* (purgation), *Niruhavasti* (cleansing decoction enema), *Anuvasana Vasti* (Nutritive enema) and *Nasya* (errhinetherapy). These are as per *Charaka*, the great ayurveda physician. The *Sushruta*, the first surgeon of the world, has added *rakta mokshana* (blood letting) after clubbing *niruhavasti* and *anuvasana vasti* as one. Then totally it will become five as per *Sushruta*. Blood letting is advised to cure blood disorders.

PRE-OPERATIVE PROCEDURES

Before the actual *panchakarma* methods of treatment are employed, the patient must be prepared. It is also necessary to assess whether the patient is fit to undergo this therapy, and also it is better to find a suitable time. These *panchakarma* treatments are employed to balance the *doshas* after flushing out the toxins from the body.

The pre-operative procedures mainly included oleation therapy and sudation therapy. With these, morbid *doshas* are brought into alimentary tract and expelled outside. Now, first we can deal with oleation therapy.

Oleation Therapy (Snehana Karma)

The patient is administered either pure ghee (clarified butter) or medicated ghee for 7 days. It serves to soothen the *doshas* and balance the digestive action. This is effective in gastric ulcer and duodenal ulcers. The use of medicated ghee is done effectively in some specific diseases. *Tiktha gritha* in a skin disease, *Dadimadigritha* in Anaemia, *Shatavari gritha* in chronic colitis. Sudation therapy, (sweat treatments) after the oleation therapy the *doshas* which are in lymphatics, blood, muscle tissue, adipose tissue, and bone marrow are liquified and drawn back to gastro-intestinal tract. The sudation therapy helps to liquify the *doshas*. This is a method of perspiring the body through steam.

Abhyanga: (Oil Massage)

Oil massage is nothing but a way of applying oil to the body with mild massage done by masseurs. This is a routine treatment not only for healthy individuals, but also for diseased people. Here, til oil (sesame oil) is used. The benefits of *abhyanga* are: soothes the skin, relieves fatigue, pains and promotes good vision, sturdy body, good sleep and good skin which will move the *doshas* into the alimentary tract. If the *dosha* involved is *kapha*, *emetics* are given, *pitta* is involved *virechana* (laxative) is administered and if the *vata* is aggravated, then, *vastis* (enemas) are given. When *pitta dosha* is aggravated, then it has to be treated by giving laxatives. This will make *doshas* flushed outside the gastro-intestinal tract and minimise the digestive fire.

CASE REPORTS

Mr. Abdul Samad, a labourer, was brought to SJIIM and H, Ayurveda Medical College, Bangalore. He was unconscious. His father Md. Azeem told me that about five months ago, his son met with an accident with head injuries. He was admitted in National Institute of Mental Health, Bangalore for five months. Intensive treatment was done in that hospital but he did not regain consciousness. In our hospital, a course of sneapana, pure ghee feeding through the spoon was started. This lasted for seven days. Then he started opening his mouth with little relaxed jaws. He was given sweating therapy with lukewarm bath. A second course of *snehapana* was started for another seven days, Then, he regained consciousness and started eating rice preparations.

Then after another sweating process, he was allowed third course of *snepanana* with increased dose of pure ghee up to seven days. As a result of this, his appetite came down to normal. The snehapana must not be continued beyond 7 days, as it will become homologous to body and acts like a food. The patient started walking and was in good health. So he was discharged after one and a half month. It is already 12 years and he is still in good health and carrying out his day-to-day duties without relapse or any complications.

ENEMA (VASTI)

Medicated enemas are given to patients. There are innumerable types of enemas mentioned in Ayurveda for several diseases. A famous orthopaedic surgeon of international repute based in Bangalore was advised immediate operation with replacement of both hip joints.

Mr. David was afraid of operation and its further probable complications. He came down to Ayurveda College Hospital at Bangalore, a pioneer institute of Ayurveda. He was advised by the principal Dr. K.R. Srikanta Murthy to see me. Later I was called to his chamber and I was advised to treat him with panchakarma, to expel and to flush out the *vata* from the large gut.

An I.A.S officer, aged fifty-five years, was diagnosed for degenerative disease of the hip bone. About 10 years ago he met with an accident and injured his hips, he suffered severe pains in both the hip joints. He underwent treatment from all orthopaedic surgeons. He was given a course of oleation, sudation therapies in addition to *kayaseka*, pouring oils over the body from a suitable height and time. Then, a course of enema (*vasti*) was also given. He was on *vata* pacifying diet for one and half months. He was sent to see the same orthopaedic surgeon, who told the patient that there was no necessity of conducting operation as the degenerative changes in the hip bones had stopped. After fifteen years, the patient is hale and healthy, with his hips intact.

To quote another case, a patient Mr. Bhat aged 45 years came to me with a history of sleeplessness (insomnia) for the last 20 years. He was a resident of Udupi. He was given a course *sirovasti* for 7 days with *ksheerabala* and *karapasatyadi* oil. The patient started getting sleep, the very day of treatment. However the treatment continued for another six days. He was advised some *vata* alleviating drugs internally for another 15 days. After 15 years he is free from insomnia. The patient was advised not to expose himself in cold climate in future. He was advised not to use *vata* aggravating diets and activities.

PANCHAKARMA INDICATIONS

In olden days panchakarma treatment was practised by Ayurvedic physicians for rich people only in India. But off late *panchakarma* is used extensively for rich and poor throughout India. In all major Ayurveda hospitals and colleges attached to Ayurveda hospitals it has become routine. Panchakarma needs to be adopted during the change of seasons. This treatment is effective, whether it is done as out-patient or as an in-patient. The treatment done as an in-patient will give more rest and peace to the patient, in addition to *panchakarma*. This treatment is employed either for healthy people to promote their health or for diseased people to get their diseases cured. After oleation and seating therapies, the emesis therapy is to be carried out.

WHEN AND WHOM TO THE EMESIS THERAPY IS EMPLOYED

When a patient is suffering from cough, cold and asthma, the emesis therapy is advocated for removing mucus and congestion. The diseases are going to be started as per Ayurveda in the stomach. As soon as the mucus is removed from the stomach, the mucus in lungs automatically stops coming.

MEDICINES USED

Oleation and perspiration must be done before the emesis therapy. A day before the emesis therapy, the mucus promoting black gram, curds and fish are given to the patients. Three to four glasses of either milk or decoction of Madhuyasti (Licorice) is given early in the morning before 10 o' clock the next day. For therapeutic vomiting, the medicines mentioned for *tamakaswasa* are given for a suitable time. This should be done under the supervision of an Ayurvedic *vaidya*. This treatment is also effective in diabetes mellitus, generalised anasarca, chronic cold, chronic loss of appetite and in skin disease.

Mr. S. Rao aged 45 years came to me with a ten-year history of chronic bronchial asthma. He was examined and investigated properly. The blood pressure, weight, respiration rate and heart rate were all recorded. He was given a course of oleation and sudation therapies for 7 days.

Then a day before the emesis therapy, *kapha* promoting food—curd, fish, blackgram were given. At 8 a.m. the next day, the patient was made to sit on a stool in *panchkarma* theatre and he was asked to drink 1 to 2 litres of milk or *Madhuyasti* decoction. Then we waited for 48 minutes. He started vomiting the milk and *doshas* including *kapha*. The vomiting stopped as soon as bile was seen in the vomit. Then for seven days, he was put on light diet of rice, gruel and Ayurveda medicines meant for bronchial asthma were given to the patient. It is already five years. He is free from attacks and he is doing his routine duties.

This treatment must be given in between the attacks. That is, it should not be tried in status Asthmatic. Before the actual vomiting therapy the prayers of Gods must be done, as a routine.

It is done to get the blessings from God and to keep the mind in peace. The patient must be in bed. Then, medicated smoking is done to liquify the *kapha dosha*.

TO WHOM THERAPEUTIC VOMITING SHOULD NOT BE DONE

Old age, childhood, heart disease, tuberculosis of the lungs, bleeding above the neck, obesity, emaciation and pregnancy.

TO WHOM PURGATION THERAPY IS ADVISED

Chronic fever, skin disease, abdominal tumour, gout, jaundice and worms.

TO WHOM IT IS NOT INDICATED

Childhren, old person, acute fever, bleeding from anus, uterus and urethra, tuberculosis of the lungs, ulcerative colitis, prolapsed rectum, diarrhoea and low digestive fire.

Mr. Damodaran, aged 35 years, had ascitis with cirrhosis of liver. He was treated in all the major hospitals without any benefit.

He was given a course of treatment—decoction of Dashamoola (10 drugs), *panchakola* (5 drugs—pippali, *pippalimula, chavya, chitraka* and *nagara*) *triphala* (*abhaya, amalaki, vibheetaki*) and *trivrit*.

To 500ml of water 50 gms of drugs are added and heated and reduced to one fourth and given at 6 a.m. and 6 p.m.

Diet: Rice is prepared with *panchakola* and water. This is given twice a day.

This treatment was continued for 15 days. The patient got complete relief. The abdomen reduced to normal. His weight was reduced. Kidneys and liver became normal on scanning.

Cow milk, castor oil, *trivrit* root (dandeloin root), mango juice, *senna, triphala* (three fruits). The treatment of therapeutic purgation for *vata pitta* is with milk and ghee. The only and best treatment for *pitta* is purgation therapy. Those who want to know more details about *panchakarma* therapy kindly read the book entitled *the Panchakarma Treatment of Ayurveda* written by this author.

ENEMAS

Enemas are a means of injecting decoctions of drugs and medicated or pure oils etc into the rectum through the anus. The purpose of introducing these things is with a specific purpose. Ayurveda believes that the origin of *vata*, the force that controls the entire movement and activities of the body, is in the large gut.

WHOM AND WHEN ENEMA
THERAPY IS INDICATED

In the following diseases, the decoction enema can be given:

Pain all over the body, pain in one organ, pain in the joints, enlargement of spleen, Fantum Tumer, Heart disease, fistula-in-Ane, head ache, and *vata vyadi* (nervous diseases).

Indications of Anuvasana Vasti (oil enema)

All nervous diseases, paralysis, hemiplegia, facial paralysis, constipation, low backache, emaciation, sciatica, arthritis and rheumatism.

Contradictions of decoction enema

Haemorrhoids, pregnancy, ascitis, diarhoea and diabetes.

Oil enema

Obesity, diabetes, less digestive fire, indigestion, coma and enlarged spleen.

For chronic constipation:

Administer 1 cup of warm sesame oil after meals as enema.

TIME OF ADMINISTRATION

Decoction enema

Early in the morning on empty stomach.

Oily enema

Immediately after meals.

TO WHOM AND WHEN ERRHINE IS GIVEN

Patients suffering from sinusitis, hoarseness of voice hemicrania, migraine, cervical spondylitis, dryness, ear, eye problems, insanity, epilepsy, jaundice, facial paralysis, toothache, lockjaw and insomnia.

WHERE IT ACTS

Errine drugs act on *prana vayu*, a type of *vata* which controls the senses, sensory, motor and also stimulates the central nervous system. Some types of *nasya* soothes the nervous systems in a comatose patient. Acute *nasyas* are given to stimulate the nervous system to get immediate consciousness. These drugs trigger the nervous system into activity.

TO WHOM IT IS NOT GIVEN

Pregnancy, menstruation, after alcohol, after bath, after food or after thirst, acute fever and bleeding diseases.

Types of Errhine therapy

1. Brihmana (nutritional)

To whom it is advised

- a) Cervical spondylosis
- b) *Sooryavarta* (migraine)
- c) Ptosis (drooping of eyelids)
- d) Loss of smell
- e) Anxiety and other nervous symptoms
- f) Paralysis—hemiplegia, facial paralysis

2. Virechana Nasya (eliminative)

It is used in *kapha* diseases, sinusitis, rhinitis, tumors, cold, epilepsy, insanity and Parkinsonism.

3. Shamana Nasya (sedative)

It is used in *pitta* disorders, hairfalls, *karnaada* (ringing in the ears) and eyes-conjunctivitis.

Drugs used: 1) Juice of asparagus root, 2) Juice of *madhuyasti* (*gotukola* juice), 3) warm milk 4) *Sneha nasya* (oily *nasya*).

Used in vata, pitta and kapha diseases, usually medicated oils are used. Dhamapana-blowing of powder into the nose in an unconsciousness state to get consciousness.

Common drugs used in Nasya

Pippali, shunti, brahmi, til oil, milk, honey, ghee, *haridra vidanga, apamarga* seeds, and randiadumetorum seeds (*madanaphala*).

Prescription

Oils: *Anutaiula, nirgunditaila, shadbindu tailam,* ghees—cows, *churnas—shatavari, brahmi, katphala, trikatu, rasa-vata vidwamsa* and *swaskuthara.*
Smoking: (medicated) *kantakari* fumes—as smoking.

How to administer Nasya

First, apply oil to head, face, neck and shoulder for about fifteen minutes. Do hot fomentation with hot water bag for about 8-0 minutes. Make the patient lie down on the bed and keep a pillow below the neck. Apply *anutaila* into one nostril about 4-8 drops by closing the other nostril and ask the patient to inhale. Gargle with hot water and apply mild fomentation. The patient must wash his face and head. He should take complete rest in bed and in calm mood.

CASE REPORT

For ENT and eye diseases and those of the head and neck, the *nasya* treatment is the best. *Prana vayu* is nothing but life which controls the sensory and motor functions of the body. When this *vayu* is deranged, it produces many diseases. To quote an example, a university professor, Mr. Brahmappa Navar, had lost his voice (aphonia), had undergone intensive course of western medicine from a medical college hospital for more than 6 months without any relief. Somebody advised him to go in for Ayurveda treatment and finally, he came to me. He was a teacher in a university college and needed his voice (tone) for teaching. Western doctors advised him to live with this ailment. He questioned the efficacy and authenticity of Ayurveda. I convinced him that there is a treatment for this. Then, I suggested a course of ksheerabala oil 8 times, medicated into his nostril in a dose of 5-6 drops into each nostril twice daily for a period of 14 days with Ayurvedic treatment for *vata*. To his great surprise he got his voice within 3 days of starting the treatment. It is already two years since he had the treatment. Till today he has no complaints. He is teaching at the university.

BLOOD LETTING

How much blood to let out

100-250ml of blood can be removed at a time. This can be repeated after a gap of 3-4 months. This is effective in skin diseases. In congestive cardiac failure also, blood letting can be instituted to relieve congestion. Mr. Rajan who was suffering from chronic skin disease, after having failed in other systems of medicine, came to me with rashes all over the body, itching sensation with scaly rashes, diagnosed as psoriasis, a resistant case of skin disease. He was given a treatment—blood letting with leeches and also blood purifying drugs as *gugglutiktha ghrita* for a one month. The pre-operative procedures of *snehana* (oleation) was done with ghee and fomentation was done. The patient became all right and he enjoyed good health afterwards.

Meditation (Dhyana)

Meditation brings calmness and mental clarity, spontaneity, simplicity and natural ease. It creates harmony, awareness and natural order. One who practises it will experience personal benefits and spiritual growth. One must choose free time especially in the morning. The place must also be comfortable and quiet.

One must sit in an upright position and be comfortable. Start your practice with keen interest.

Close your eyes and breath naturally and look into the space in between your eyebrows. Concentrate on it and be happy and feel thankful for the gift of life and expand your consciousness. You can pray to God now. This should be very slow. Then, you can recite *mantras* boldly and loudly. You can conclude your practice after bringing

awareness of your feeling, thoughts, senses and feeling
you have to sit for a minute for smooth transition of inner
focusing to outer environment.

If you have got special things to examine, then this
must be done during conclusion of meditation. This
practice is to be done for 2-5 minutes. In the process the
body will be relaxed and the mind will be quiet.

Benefits of meditation: Youthful energy and vitality.
Profound change in the body and mind. There is another
way of meditation, which also brings blessings.

CASE REPORT

Mr. Manjunath, aged 5 years, has 170/120 mm of high
blood pressure. He was on antihypertensive drugs
without any relief. He came to me for consultation. I
checked up his blood pressure. I advised him a course of
meditation with minimum Ayurveda drugs. After 15 days
of meditation his blood pressure came down to normal.
Then, oral drugs were stopped and he was informed to
do meditation for another 6 months. He is free from high
blood pressure even after 8 years.

Breathing is life's energy, which has two units—
inspiration, taking oxygen inside and expiration, expelling
carbon dioxide outside. Inspiration is cold, whereas
expiration is warm. The cosmic sound ohm-hum and female
energy is on during inhale the female cosmic consciousness
from individual consciousness. These vibrations are one
with life of breathing one has to go beyond time and space
cause and effect unlimitedly and finally consciousness
dilate and expand to maximum. *Samadhi* is ultimate union
of individual consciousness to cosmic consciousness,
equilibrium of body and the lightest equilibrium of body
and mind.

Prof. B. Ramamurthy, a neuro surgeon, Chennai, has
proved that through meditation alphawaves will be

increased and they are useful in reducing high blood pressure and epilep.

A person who meditates regularly will get these benefits. So meditation must be practised under a teacher. One cannot practise by going through a book. *Mantras* are primordial sounds which vibrate in one's mind and body. They later lead on to matter to energy finally after practice of *mantras* the mind will move into quantum level. With all these *mantras* the nature vibrates will have a definite influence on healing the body and mind. The word quantum is derived from Latin which means how much. The finest of the body is made of atom which is further divided. Blood, bone, muscle are all made up of tissues ending finest atoms. The primordial sounds are transmitted from a trained meditator to another person. The *prana* is the first unit of cosmic life before which the natural order is provided. Sound vibrations are effective in relieving pains, anginapectoris.

INTRODUCTION TO THE MIND

Mind is an inseparable union of the body, sensory and motor organs of the body and the soul. *Veda* means knowledge, which is acquired through the mind and sense organs. Hence the mind plays a major and prominent role. The *dravya* is a substance, which may be either animate (living) and inanimate (non-living). The following are the nine substances.

Akasha (space), *agni* (fire), *vayu* (air), *prithvi* (earth), *jala* (water), *atma* (soul), *manas* (Mind), *dik* (direction) and *kala* (time). Space is the various spaces of the body. Air is the subtle and gross movements. Fire (digestive) causes digestion and assimilation. Water maintains fluid balance. Earth helps in shaping the body. Mind represents mental faculties. Soul is the ego or intellect. Time represents the living body and direction reveals the extension of space and time.

QUALITIES OF MIND

Mind possesses the same qualities as other substances. In addition to anutva and *ekatva*. More so, the qualities of *viz satwa*, *rajas* and *tamas*.

Mind has got dual qualities which are quite opposite to each other. The gunas of *satva* on one side and *rajas* and *tamas* on the other side. The *satya* qualities will make a man of good character with good qualities. The *rajas* and *tamas* will make a bad and undesirable man with bad temperament and activities.

Qualities of Satva	Qualities of Rajas and Tamas
1. Simplicity	1. Anger
2. Brahmacharya	2. Aversion
3. Bravery	3. Pomp and show
4. Firmness	4. Boasting
5. Equality of mind	5. Lethargy
	6. Worry

Satva: It is a quality of mind, which is capable of acquiring knowledge, purity of thought, word, deed and wisdom.
Rajas: It is a quality of mind, which is not useful to individual. It goes into early vitiation and disturbance of other two properties. It is an initiator. This produces desire and memory.
Tamas: It produces soothening, calming effect on the body. A balance of all the three *gunas* or qualities is essential for a healthy state of mind and body.

There are stimuli that come into contact with the human body as such the sense of hearing, sense of vision, sense of touch, sense of smell and taste. After these come into contact with the body, the intellect ego and memory and other aspects of mind like reasoning, thinking, deduction and rationalisation come into function. The mind plays an important role. In secure *dharma*, *arth*, *kama* and salvation, one has to have a hale and healthy body and mind. In order to experience 20 qualities which are physical in nature, the mind is in dire need in their perception.

The *atmik gunas* indicate the presence of soul in the body.

- intellect, grasping memory, reason, perception, retention and understanding.
- Desires, wishes, longing and craving
- Hatred, dislike and revulsion
- Happiness due to aversion of desires
- Endeavour and effort

The above qualities of mind are also there, in addition to 20 physical qualities of the body.

- Superiority and inferiority are also present.
- The *satwa* is predominant of *akasha*.
- The *rajas* is predominant of *vayu*.
- The *tamas* is predominant of *prithvi*.

In order to keep the body and mind in equillbrium, it is necessary the three pillars i.e. three *doshas* and three supporting pillars—food, sleep and celibacy—must be in equilibrium. The three *gunas* are influenced by the food that we take. The food after digestion will be converted into gross, which nourishes the body, tissues and cells, and subtle, which nourishes the mind, and the excretas will be excreted out, as urine, faeces and sweat.

Manasika Prakriti: The Psychological Constitution

This is the result of the activities of the three *gunas* at the time of conception with sperm and ovum. The mental situation and status of the parents predispose the foetus. The mental state of a person is divided into three types—satva, *rajas* and *tamas*.

A. Satwa: There are seven types.

1. Brahma type: When a person is pure, has self-control, is devoted to truth, has a discriminating mind is endowed with source of knowledge, reasoning, understanding, power of exposition, unfailing memory and free from desire, greed, anger, conceit, infatuation, dejection, intolerance and envy. He will have imbalance of mind and his opinions are respected by all people, even though some differ with him in some judgements opinion.

2. Arsha type: Arsha type of person will have the following attributes. Devoted to sacrifice, study offerings, celibacy, hospitable, devoid of attachments, conceit, hate, infatuation, anger, greed, endowed with eloquence, genius and understanding.

Arshas have written books on sciences, *vedas* music and yoga etc. These people will engage themselves in meditation, pursuit of knowledge starting centres of knowledge for its dessemination.

3. Indra type: Indra is the king of Gods. But here a man who is gifted with lordship with authoritative speech, perform sacrifices, is brave, energetic, possessing foresight and devoted to virtue, wealth and sensual pleasures.

4. Yama type: Yama type of person does right things, is unassailable, constantly alert, industrious, has a good memory, is free from attachment, hate, infatuation and envy.

5. Varuna type: This type of person is courageous, intolerant, valiant, performs sacrifices, is fond of water, aquatic sport, clean and clearcut actions, expresses anger, pleasure of appreciation on the spot in an articulate way. Varuna is a diety who governs water.

6. Kubera type: Kubera is the treasurer of Gods. He commands status, luxury, honour, attendants, who believe in pursuit of wealth, pleasures and practice of virtue. He is clean and loves sensual pleasures.

7. Gandharva type: Gandharva type of person is fond of dancing, music, song, praise, well versed in poetry, ballads, history, legends, loves fragrance, garlands, scents, ornaments, women, recreation, free from envy and hatred.

Gandharva has links with Gods. He loves good life, colourful bright clothes, scents, company of ladies, and he is a happy person.

B. Rajas: Whenever a person is short tempered, violent, envious, pitiless, ruthless, volatile and eats heavy meal with big belly.

1. Asura type: Rajas is held responsible for movement, initiation and activity. Those type of a person is impatient, emotional and over active.

2. Rakshasa type: Rakshas type of person possesses anger and is intolerant, cruel, does not believe in code of conduct, eats too much, loves meat, loves sleep and he does not get fatigued easily. These people will go revengful and likes his own sleep and food. They do not believe in ethics.

3. Pishacha type: He eats too much food, is of easy virtue, loves ladies, loneliness, unclean and is obnoxious. His behaviour is abnormal and he is shameless.

4. Sarpa type: (sarpa-snake) Is brave when angry but usually coward in nature. He does not get tired easily, loves food and is a fast eater. He is industrious in nature.

5. Preta type: (Preta-demon) He lives for food, is envious, possessive, covetous, and hates work. These type of people are immature, lack of motive, and self-confidence.

6. Shakuna type: These type of people are usually preoccupied with gratification of sexual desire and have short relationships. They enjoy the food, drinks and are fickle in nature. They are intolerant, and do not like to think about their future. These people are like birds. They do not plan their future.

C. Types of tamas: These type of people are unintelligent dull, disrespectful, with excess sexual drive and eating habits. They behave like animals, respectful, dull, disgusting in his attitude and behaviour and food habits. He is somnolent and unfit for any responsible job. They are fit as manual labourers.

3. Matsya type: (Matsya-fish)These type of people live in fear, are stupid, unintelligent, greedy for food, persistent for likes or dislikes, are greedy, have an unstable mind, move constantly long distance, like water to drink. They are more or less salesmen. They have to work under a supervisor.

4. Vanaspatya type: These type of people are lazy, fit for only eating food and they are devoid of any mental faculties. They are misfit for any job.

The above sixteen types are known as psychological constitutions. People who are living in this world of macrocosm, must be one of the above types. For appointments, education and other fields, the above parameters will be naturally of great help.

TREATMENT OF MENTAL DISEASES

Ayurveda has laid more stress on proper diet, correct behaviour attending to natural urges, control of psychological activity, observing daily and seasonal regimen to prevent the diseases and to protect the health.

Ayurveda pleads that a state of vitiated *doshas*, digestive fire, tissue and excreta into a proper equilibrium will bring the person to healthy state of body and mind. The health of a person, spiritual, physical and mental, must be made into harmony of equilibrium. The treatment of mental diseases needs not only medicine but it comprises, assurance, counselling, suggestion, diet, chanting of suitable *mantras*, wearing of amulets, offering oblations and so on.

The management of mental disorders comes under three headings.

  i) *Daivavyapasraya*
 ii) *Satyavajaya*
iii) *Yuktivyapasraya.*

i) Daivavyapasraya consists of chanting of *mantras* and performing various sacrifices. It includes offering of herbs along with various ingredients—rice, ghee, resins are all offered to fire. Fasting, observation of eating certain things and avoiding prayers to deities, atonement (Prayashitta) play a major role in controlling *rajas* and *tamas* activity of mind and to promote *satwa* predominance to get a healthy state of mind and body.

ii) Satvavajaya: The abnormal mental activity is controlled by code of conduct (*yama*), yogic pastures (*asana*) and balanced breathing (*pranaama*). These are essential for maintaining balance of mind and body.

iii) Yuktivyapasraya: It consists of proper use of medicines and diet. It includes *shamana* (palliative) and *shodhana* (pentad of purificatory procedures). The internal use of *brahmi* (bacopa monieri), *jatamamsi* (nardostachyis jatamamsi), *khurasania jawan* (hyocymus niger), *lashuna* (allivum sativum), *hingu* (ferula asafoetida) and ghee is useful in mental disorders. Femugation and *panchagavya* (a mixture of cow's milk, curd, urine, ghee and cow dung) has a prominent place in the treatment of epilepsy (*apasmara*) and insanity (*unmada*).

The secondary treatments include *panchakarma* therapies *viz* irrigation of oils, milk, buttermilk over the head, (*sirodhara*), keeping of medicated oil over the head in a leather cap (*sirovasti*), keeping of oils on the vertix of the head (*siropichu*). These treatments must be done under the guidance and strict supervision of an Ayurveda physician. There must be a smooth and cordial rapport between the *vaidya* and the patient in all these treatments, for their success and effectiveness.

Intellect promoting formulas

Ayurveda therapeutics promote strength of body and immunity to diseases by increasing the resistance of the patient.

1. The intellect promoting drugs as fresh juice of centella asciatica (*mandookaparni*).
2. The powder of the stem of glycyrrhiza globra (*yastimadhu*) along with cow's milk.
3. The fresh juice of stem of tinosporacordifolia (*guduchi*).
4. The root past of clitoriaternatia (*aparijita*).

These drugs are life promoting, disease alleviating, strength promoting, promotion of digestive fibre, voice, complexion memory and intellect.

The important thing is to make the patient aware of his capacity, strength, weakness, and so on to balance the mind for a healthy state of mind and body.

7)	Detachment	7)	Greed for power
8)	Faith is God	8)	Egoism
9)	Truth	9)	Atheism
10)	Silence	10)	Fear
11)	Contentment	11)	Desires
12)	Humility	12)	Doubling his own mind
13)	Sharpness	13)	Jumps with joy
14)	Quickness	14)	Likes travel and sight seeing
15)	Aloof in nature	15)	Talkative
16)	Tolerance	16)	Talking false matters
17)	Adaptability	17)	Lust
		18)	Passion

The ultimate goal of meditation is to bring the *Rajas* and *tamas* into a state of *satwa*, which is required for calmnes, contentment, detachment, sharpness, quickness and tolerance. Meditation is done in Brahma Muhurtam.

Seated on a good plank, with a lamp lit with oil. For good fragrance and lit incense sticks.

The cure of cancer or any dreaded disease is possible due to the effect of finest vibrations acting on the mind and body.

Sound and medicine

It is necessary to say that sound waves work as medicines. These are called primordial sounds. The sages of Ayurveda have described the union of two electrons and which is boundary a helium atom these sounds are can be either chanted loudly or spoken by a person to others. The ohm-mental sound is more powerful. The disease is the defect in transmission of its obstruction.

Pulse diagnosis

Ayurveda postulates that all the activities of the body and mind are perceived through pulse reading. All the activities of the body, cells, tissues and organs are in close link with heart through the blood stream, which will be reflected in the pulse. Hence, pulse reading will give us an account of the health or diseases and the state of a person. Pulse reading is of paramount importance in Ayurved for diagnosis of any disease commencing from fever to AIDS. It is the gateway for a mechanical body. The Ayurvedic doctor palpates the pulse at the wrist and gives the diagnosis. This science of pulse science (*Nadivijana*) was very popular in olden days. A patient, Sridhar came with a complaint of pain in the foot. On examination of the pulse of the patient only, the patient was told that he had an accident 10 years ago and the back pain started, later it moved to legs. Then he was prescribed Ayurveda medicines. It was cured once for all. You can see several bands of diseases in one pulse only, diseases of small gut, large gut, spleen, liver, kidney or the brain are also diagnosed through the reading of pulse. Nature has made a tremendous arrangement. No advanced techniques of science may be in a position to make such subtle and minute arrangements. The pathological changes that are going to take place can be recorded in pulse reading. The balance or imbalance of the *doshas* and the tissues or organs can be read daily. The changes in the physical and mechanical body can be recorded by physical reading of the pulse.

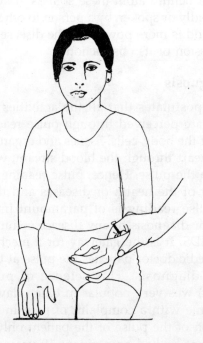

There are eight methods of diagnosis and pulse is one of them. In a healthy person pulse helps us to trace the nature of constitution viz. *vata* and *kapha*. The *rasa*, the essence of panchabhautic food, is later converted into blood and circulates all over the body. So, one must know the movement of the *rasa*. The motion is atomic (molecular) level or cellular level or at the quantum level of the body. The sound waves are transmitted through the blood stream. One must learn the art of reading the pulse from a competent Ayurveda physician.

How to read pulse: Normally, pulse reading is done at radial artery, very near the wrist joint with the help of thumbs. Pulse can be felt in the neck or above the wrist joint with the help of thumbs. It can be felt in the neck or above the ankle joint or in the big toe. The patient must be in a relaxed mood, physically and mentally. After passing urine and faeces, usually the right hand pulse is used for recording the male, the three fingers, index finger, middle finger and the ring finger are use to detect the nature of health or disease. The points of index middle and ring finger represent *vatadosha, pittadosha* and *kapha dosha* respectively.

Vata type of pulse will be like a leech movement or snake movement. It is very fast and light.

Pitta type of pulse will be like the movement of frog or crow. Its movement is quick and sharp.

Kapha type of pulse resembles the movement of a swan or dove. The speed is slow and heavy. The pulse is feeble and slow in the following conditions:

1. Haemorrhage-bleedings
2. Psychological disease—depression, agitation, stress and worries.
3. Internal haemorrhage: intestinal, vaginal.
4. Curable disease—dull, cutting, trembling, fearing
5. In diabetes, pulse is minute and dull. The right arm radial artery is used for males and left arm for the female.

Contraindications of pulse reading

1. After food
2. After sun bath
3. After alcohol
4. After heavy work
5. After massage
6. After exposure to fire

Usage of pulse reading

On superficial touch of right radial pulse, one can detect the defects of the large intestine, gall bladder and pericardium. On deep touch of pulse of right hand, you can detect the disorder of lungs, liver and three *doshas*— Vata, *pitta* and *kapha*.

On superficial touch of left pulse, one can detect the defects of small gut, stomach and bladder. On deep touch of left radial touch, you can find the defects of heart, spleen and kidney.

The pulse will be slow in the morning, gets aggravated in the noon and more in the *vata* period. The fingertips contain 13000 nerve endings, which will have direct link with the brain during pulse reading.

Pulse reading of Ayurveda will be more precise and accurate in diagnosis by a trained and qualified Ayurveda physician than any gadgets of the modern world.

Pulse-reading

When pulse reading is not done—after food, after massage, after exercise, after sex, after bath, after alcoholic drink and after sun bath.

Pulse rate and age: 160 per minute, afterbirth 140 per minute, 3-7 years 95 per minute, 8-14 yrs 80 per minute, adult 72 per minute, old age 65-70 per minute, at the time of death—160 per minute. Changes in pulse reading are seen in different times of the day and also when one is hungry and excited.

Awakening the marmas

These marmas are felt through tactile sensation.

There are three vital *marmas* present in the body, viz head, heart and bladder. The *marmas* are stimulated or awakened by several ways. The *siromarma* (vital *marma* in the head) will be soothened by *dhara* treatment. The *dhara* is nothing but irrigation of the head with suitable oils at a distance of 4 inches, from one to one and half an hours and reduced to one hour. This method is employed to make the head adjust to treatment. This kind of treatment is effective in sleeplessness and epilepsy, and other mental diseases.

Marma therapeutics

Marma is nothing but a vital point of the body. In Ayurveda there are 107 invisible *marmas*. Out of them three are called vital points. When these points are injured, then death is a certainty. So one has to guard these places carefully and cautiously.

In our body, there are thousands of nerve endings in each and every part which connects the mind from the mechanical body. If a needle is pricked on our skin, which transmits message to the brain through the nerve endings and immediately the needle will be removed. Usually warm oils are used. The seat of *vata* is in the skin. Doing *abhyanga* (oil application with mild massage) to body and head will stimulate the circulation and soothens the nerve system. For maintaining harmony and balance of *vata dosha* these methods are beneficial. Transcendental meditation will trigger the three major *marmas*, which in turn stimulate the smaller *marmas* into activity. The bliss thereapy is helpful in promoting stimulation of these invisible *marmas*.

Importance of marma in treatment

These marmas are the energy center of quantum mechanical body. *Marma* means, hidden or secret. Even in

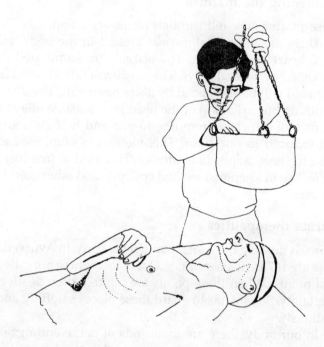

Ayurveda, the science of acupuncture is there. Massage is done on the *marma* points in order to restore and balance the normal function or relax the contracted part or muscle. Each *marma* is an anatomical area. *Marma* points are massaged with the help of a thumb in small, clockwise, gentle, moving outward and later backward direction. Then, increase the pressure slowly and decrease and do massage in circular movement 3-5 times in joints of the body.

To *siras*, *hridays* and *vast*, massage with *vata* pacifying oils on the front of the foot and palm and also the head and body. This will soften the *vata* and help to keep its balance. The *hridaya* marma is located in the chest and the *vasti marma* is situated below the umbilicus and *siro marma* is located in between the eyebrows. Whenever there is a headache, then smooth circular massage with oil should be done on the head for relief. If the patient has bowel problems, it is better to massage on the *vasti* vital point in the circular way. The *marma* therapy must be learnt under a trained Ayurveda physician.

Bliss therapy

This therapy is for joy, happiness and pleasantness of mind.

The purpose of life is purler for securing health, happiness and joy. Laughter is the best medicine is an adage. So one must keep his quantum mechanical body and mind joyful. This requires *satvic* mind when people use milk, ghee, peaceful bent of mind through meditation. Spiritual bent of activities will make diseases like high blood pressure vanished by this way of life. Blissful life is the order of the day. The health, physical, beauty and ultimate success are treated and termed as happiness by western people. But, of late, they are realising the truth of original bliss through *satvic* way and foods and living through different types of meditation. Westerners have learnt meditation techniques and they are practising. People with cancer therapy, who undergo meditation with conventional treatment get relief quickly. As a matter of fact, cancer therapy with ayurveda medicine, along with meditation has given astounding and unexpected results. Many cases which fail in other systems of medicine have been treated successfully with Ayurveda along with meditation.

Bliss and its natural phenomena

When three *doshas* are in a balanced state, they will produce spontaneous joy.

Vata: Alert, cheerful, optimistic, flexible and stimulating.
Pitta: Clear minded, contended, joyful and pleasant.

Kapha: Strong, steady, courageous, generous, serene and affectionate.

Vata is the main force just as wind which moves the clouds from one place to another, which controls the *pitta* and *kapha* in the body. All the activities of the cells, tissues, organs, body and mind are controlled by *vata*. It is like a main switch of the electricity in town. As soon as its switch is on all the substations and house lights and currents will be generated. *Vata* is compared to nervous system. All the messages and impulses are sent through the nervous *vata*. All the three *doshas* should be balanced to get health, which is necessary to get *ananda* (bliss) in our life. The balance of digestive fire, three *doshas*, all the seven *dhatus*, (tissues) and *malas*, urine, faeces and sweat etc. and clarity of mind with pleasantness are necessary for obtaining blissful joy and happiness. This is also seen when a person gets success and wealth. A person gets success and wealth through stages of spiritual growth. It starts from full enlightenment. God, consciousness, cosmic consciousness, dysfunctional self-consciousness leading to unconsciousness. Every soul is awakened from unconsciousness to self knowledge and realisation to oneness in God. The ways of right living and spirtitual practice speed up their process.

Super fluidity comes from an eccentric matter of super fluids. This is the discovery of physicists. It creates an atmosphere of effortless, frictionless moods in a usual state of meditation. It requires concentration of mind.

This bliss therapeutic technique must be learnt under an able Ayurveda doctor or a teacher, before teaching the technique one should be experienced in treating several cases and several types of anxiety and depression or disorders related to them.

Aroma therapy *(Balancing doshas through smell)*

The *panchabuthas* are necessary for the growth of man. It is to say he is constituted by it. So also the *panchendriyas* of the quantum mechanical body, smell is one of them. The touch of a person's skin will be in the form of vibrations. This is true of even *doshas*.

Vata: Touch and hearing
Pitta: Sight
Kapha: Smell and taste

If a person is of *vata* constitution, then he will be very lean and thin in build.

The *pitta* predominance constitution cannot bear sunlight continuously, cannot be exposed to heat in the kitchen or in the factory. They have light hair, light skin and world beauty. In the *kapha* constitution predominance will have a feeling of smell and taste of the food. These people love the earth, wealth and nature.

Seeing through full moon and walking in winter are stated to be good for the *pitta dosha*. So basing on the aroma therapy patient also feels delighted and enlightened in body and mind.

The role of the aromas in tridosha

Ayurveda has given six *rasas* or tastes in our food that we consume daily *viz* sweet, sour, salt, pungent astringent and bitter.

Sweet is in sugar, sour is in tamarind, pungent is in red chillies, astringent is in pomegranate and bitter is bitter gourd. Salt is present in common salt.

For pacifying *vata dosha*, sweet foods are required. It also hold good for *pitta*. The sweet smell of lactose is also good for *vata*. The pungent, sour and salt foods aggravate *pitta* in the body, the sour smell also has the same effect as well as putrid smell.

Cold atmospheric smell will aggravate *vata* and *kapha*. Pungent, bitter and astringent foods will aggravate *vata dosha*.

The speciality of the nose is that it smells the food. The olfactory nerve situated inside the mucous membrane of the nose does this work. These nerves have the power to regenerate once in 21 days approximately. The smell is transmitted into the hypothalamus situated in the brain through cells of olfactory nerves. The same type of transmission of body temperature, hunger, thirst, sexual instinct and so on will be carried to the centre, in hypothalamus. The vital centres as respiratory and heart centre are also situated in fourth ventricle of the brain.

The vomiting centre, heat centre and sleep centre etc. are also situated in the fourth ventricle of the brain. Happiness and unhappiness are also experienced in the brain. These are also controlled by sensory and motor systems. If an individual falls on the back of the head (occipit), naturally there will be a stroke or sudden death due to pressure on these vital centres.

Aroma therapy for vata imbalance

The *vata* is having dry light cold suitable and mobile. So one has to use antiproperties of *vata*, this is to say sweet, sour and salty. The aggravated *vata* will produce rough dry skin, emaciation and liking for hot things. Aroma therapy is beneficial in the following diseases:

Depression, stress, arthritis, back ache, muscle ache, headaches, sinusitis, skin diseases, bronchial asthma, insomnia, metabolic and digestive problems.

Vata is balanced with the following aromas:

Sweet, sour, warm, aromas of orange, basil, clove, spices, calamus and camphor.

Pitta dosha is balanced by a mixture of cool and sweet aromas, rose, catrip, jasmine, sandal wood, pepper, peppermint and coriander. **Kapha dosha** is balanced with warm aromas clove, pungent spices, eucalyptus, camphor, lemongrass, cinnamon and garlic.

Bedtime aromas. The aroma filled in vessels can be kept in chamber where one sleeps. It is conducive to produce sleep. A patient who has a cough due to *kapha* is pacified by the use of *kapha* alleviating oil for inhalation. The sweet smelling warm oil is also used for inhalation and yields good results.

Aroma therapy is learned from a teacher of Ayurveda or an Ayurvedic physician.

Eucalyptus oil is poured into warm water in a vessel or pot. Sometimes clove oil is also useful for this malady and used to inhale through the nose.

Gandharva music therapy of India

Gandharva music has been in India since times immemorial. This music cools the brain and also balances high blood pressure. It keeps the mind calm and tranquil.

Role of Gandharva music as medicine

Sounds have got a definite effect on our mechanical body. Loud sounds produce stress, hypertension, strain and sleeplessness.

But Gandharva music with suitable ragas or tones, if played, will give a resounding benefit to the sufferers. The role of music in treating several diseases was demonstrated by Sri Ganapathi Sachidananda Swamiji of Mysore. The gandharva music, if played slowly, is useful in pacifying *vata dosha*, but if the sounds of the music are accentuated, then it vibrates more and produces more pulse and blood pressure. The different tones or ragas will have different actions on *doshas*, as we have already seen that the different tases like sweet, sour, bitter, astringent, salt and pungent will pacify the *doshas*, so also the sense of smell will pacify the *doshas* as the different colours do it. These ragas of music are different in morning, evening, noon and night etc. The sound waves are also going to help the growth of the plants. These are also proved scientifically.

These types of the treatment are in vogue in India. Many people are getting relief out of it. Music discs and tapes are available in the market for particular indications. Some western doctors have introduced it recently in Bangalore.

These types of the treatment are in vogue in India. Many people are getting relief out of it. Music discs and tapes are available in the market for particular indications. Some western doctors have introduced it recently in Bangalore.

Utility of Gandharva music

The melodies of Gandharva music are useful in:
1. Convalescence period for the speedy recovery
2. Before going to bed to get good sleep
3. As soon as one wakes up in the morning
4. After dinner to make it settle down cool and calmly.

Method or procedure

The person must close his eyes and concentrate on the Gandharva music for a specific period 1-5 minutes. If you listen to Gandharva music before meals then it not only settles your food but also pacifies vata and balances it.

Mode of action

There are sounds of music, which vibrates in atmosphere and reflects on the mind and body. People who work all day in a pool of stress and strain, when they go back to their house, which is calm will be of solace of peace and tranquility and pleasantness of the mind will be observed. It is a way for healthy living.

These techniques of the therapy must be learnt under a trained Ayurvedic doctor.

Raga is nothing but same thing which produces pleasantness and happiness in the mind. Sangeetha (the music) is *bramhanda*. The speaking is started from *nada*. *Nada* is started with *shruthi, swara*. This was originated by Brahma with ohmkara. Gandharva *veda* is *upaveda* of *sama veda*.

Swaras are of seven types. In Ayurveda, *nada* treatment is advocated. Sound vibrat.ons have a definite impact on the health of a man. Smt. Sangamithra, wife of Mr. Arunkumar Devanath is conducting sound treatment (*sangeetha*) in America. The *sangeetha* sounds vibration are transmitted through the ears into the brain, as an electric energy. This stimulates the limbric system in hypothalamus. There is interrelation between the *sangeetha* and hormones. Brain mapping will help to identify the effect of *sangeetha* or music on the brain. By hearing the sound of music knowledge, mathematics, vocabulary will be accentuated and the intellectual power will be increased. Music sounds waves will have an effect on left and right hemisphere of the brain and diseases arising out of these will be controlled and cured.

Music for dental extract

Recorded music is played before the actual extraction of the teeth. The patient will have no pain. Recently in Bangalore, a cassette of music for the relief of *vata, pitta* and *kapha* was released for public. High blood pressure is controlled by music. It helps to promote proper circulation of blood. The respiration and pain is relieved.

An American has published a book on the role of music in the diseases.

Efficacy of music therapy after operations

After operations of abdomen, biopsy, abortions, kidneys, cancer, along with drugs, if music therapy is adopted, it will lessen the dose of pain killers and their side effects. Head phones are advisable to hear the music as they will hinder nuisance to public.

Resistance power

When the natural resistance power is perfect in the man, this will be more. When music sounds and its vibrations reach the brain, so also it increases the cortisone hormone level will be decreased. The sitar music of Ravi Shanker has increased cortisone, the resistance power and 3 factors which reduce resistance power were absent. Music must be good to hear to ears and it cools the brain. The different types of music cure different types of diseases.

Music in the morning, cools the brain. Shastric music is found to be more effective in diseases. The Mohanraga, Kamboji, Behag, nadas are more powerful in diseases. The Anandabyravi is powerful in reducing high blood pressure. Hindola, Bhupathi, Vasantha, Kanda, Nilambari, Asaveru music will bring the agitated brain to peace. Navagrapha music of Muthuswamy Dikshitar reduces pain in abdomen. For insanity the Saranga *raga* does good, Todi and Shivarangini are useful in psychiatric diseases. The morning *suprabhata* prayer is also good for health of body and mind.

Need for education of music

There need not be education of music to patients. Mr. Smith working in an American company in India used to ill-treat a lady staff. Music was used daily in his office in the morning for about half an hour which resulted in calming down of the mood of the proprietor. Secondly, Akber, a researcher, who was fed up with his work was put on music therapy and became perfectly alright.

Benefit of music to people

1. Mind be peaceful
2. Clear tone is produced
3. Activity increases
4. Memory increases
5. Resistance power increases
6. The power of intellect improved
7. The septic hormones get destroyed
8. It increases health and age.

Primordial sounds

Everybody has roots reaching deep into primordial nature of the cosmos. These are obscured by the knots tied by over-ego in our mind-body-soul complex. This realisation is by means of an awakening of divine power lying hidden in the mind body and soul complex. This power is entitled as Kundalini, because it is coiled like a spiral. The *chakras* are the major centre of psychic energy situated all along the vertebra (spinal) column is the complex of mind body and soul complex. There are seven *chakras* according to Hindus. The first five corresponds to *prithvi* (earth), *ap* (water), *tejas* (fire), *vayu* (air) and *akasa* (space). The sixth one corresponds to *manas* or Mind. The seventh *chakra* is situated in awakening and self-realisation. The tantric practices promote and trigger the dormant power of the 'kundalini' through the *chakras*, which is the seat of psychic energy.

One can manipulate the subtle layers of the mind with the help of primordial sounds. Ayurveda has described the finest sounds, which is nature's gift. All the things of the universe are made up of matter and energy like human beings, water, trees, rocks and sun, moon and stars of the ether. In the innermost and deepest level of the world, one can find the quantum field. It is the contribution of physicist. It is the smallest of electricity, light or other things, which are existing in the natural world. These are connected by unbounded quantum. The transistors, conductors, super-conductors, laser, X-rays are practical applications of the quantum fields. This is in and around our nature. This is possible in the mind of man. It can be experienced through transcendental meditation as migraine.

Primordial sounds are nothing but finest vibrations, which will set right the cells and brain impulses. The patient got relief with this treatment and he was advised to continue for another 6 months. His migraine disappeared once and for all. The degree of action of primordial sounds differ from individual to individual.

Ayurveda, a medical science of more than five thousand years, has practiced this medical line of treatment for the benefit of human beings. This must also be learnt from an Ayurvedic doctor.

Chapter Eight

GOODBYE TO ADDICTIONS FOR A HEALTHY LIVING

We are living in the age of super civilisation. The trend is more towards drinking, smoking and chewing of addictive drugs.

The number has swelled into many thousands and lacs. The adult's addiction lead on to addictions in the younger generation. They do not know the evil effects of drinking alcohol and smoking.

Alcohol in moderate amount after food is a tonic. It does not produce liver damage, tuberculosis of the lungs, cancer of the liver and so on. Innumerable rehabilitation centres have invested crores of rupees. This is not going to solve this problem.

Heavy drinkers must be made to give up this bad habit. Continuous drinking leads to loss of appetite, liver dysfunction and later liver cirrhosis.

Smoking

Smoking produces dryness in the respiratory tract. One can understand that the lungs which are made up of alveoli of muscle tissues not require much time for getting putrification leading to cough, pneumonia, tuberculosis, chronic bronchitis, asthma and in some cases, it leads to cancer of the lung. Not all the smokers get cancer, as there is resistance to infection, that is to say their immunity is strong. So such people do not suffer from it soon.

The younger age groups are being attracted towards smoking. This is a social stigma and every one thinks that one is superior to others, because he smokes. This is a false prestige and it should be stopped.

Brown sugar

Then comes the brown sugar. This industry flourishes in the young age students and young adults. They cannot live without it. They are living on it. They cannot miss a day without it, because it is a habit forming drug.

Governments and the W.H.O are trying their best to remove this stigma from the people. Crores of rupees are being spent on it. Proper education regarding the bad effects of drinking, either hot drinks or beers and smoking and eating brown sugar and so on must be given to the public.

Role of Ayurveda in addicted patients

Ayurveda has its own role in balancing the initiated memory which is called *smriti*. Addicted patients lose memory. Each and every cell in the body is subjected to misuse by these bad habits. One has to make many arrangements, change of place and education regarding drug abuse.

Meditation

In chronic alcoholics, chronic drug addicts and chronic smokers, it is difficult to retrace their bad habits to abstain from these evil habits. However, an attempt should be made to pursue the path of non-alcoholic, non drug and no smoking place in the society through regular meditation. It will take six months to one year to get fruitful results. In India, some states have already banned smoking in public places. The central government has also banned smoking in offices and public places.

Smoking and drinking in public places must be prohibited. To some extent, this addiction will be reduced. Best thing would be to train drug addicts to practise transcendental meditation. The continuous practice of this meditation will awaken the lost memory in the brain cells. This experimental trail has been successfully implemented in the centres of health in foreign countries, where Maharshi International Institutions have their centres. In India also it is being tried successfully in some centres.

Involvement of doshas in addiction

The addicted people will have self-maintaining mechanism inside their body. The normal balance of the mechanism is at stake. Especially in chronic alcoholics, smokers and drug addicts, there will be irreparable imbalance of this mechanism. In all of these, the *doshas* will be automatically aggravated. The *pitta dosha* is seen more aggravated and produce a flushed skin, thirst and abnormal sweating, irritation and abnormal violence and digestive disorders. The *vata dosha* will control the habit of drinking and smoking, as these are under its control. Finally the entire nervous system will be at bay, and all its functions will be distorted and deranged.

There are four stages of alcoholism.

In its initial stages the patient gets intellect, memory and love to people. He gets pleasantness of mind. He gets good sleep and sex interest. He reads books with interest and sings well.

In the second stage of alcoholism, patients get dull memory, sound and behaves like a drunkard. He feels lethargic. He cannot differentiate good from bad:

In the third stage, the man loses his intellect and control of his senses. He insults his elders and teachers. He eats dirty food.

In the fourth stage the person becomes unconscious. He loses control over his brain.

To whom the alcohol is prohibited

People who are excited, timid, thirsty, sorrowful, exhausted, long walk or tiresome work, obstruction to natural urges, excessive intake of food and water and indigestion.

The following symptoms and signs of *vata* addiction and its derangement are under:

1. Tremor-*kampavata*
2. Parkinson's disease
3. Mental deterioration.

These are seen in three stages viz mild, moderate and serious.

1. Mild changes

Loss of memory, loss of concentration, more worries, restlessness, differed thoughts and loss of freshness.

2. Moderate changes

Nervousness—tremor in hands, anxiety, loss of appetite, impaired thinking, feels tired—physically, loss of physical coordination and loss of sleep.

3. Serious changes

Severe nervousness—shaking of hands and head, loss of hunger, delusions and hallucinations. Chronic alcoholics and drug addicts will naturally go into the state of too much *vata* aggravation. The schizophrenic type of activities are nothing but mental changes due to *vata* vitiation at its highest level.

Mild and moderate changes in a chronic alcoholic and chronic drug addicts are treatable. The changes leading to serious imbalance of *vata* to the extreme heights are not at all easily treatable. Mild changes result in mild imbalance of *doshas*. So also, moderate changes will have moderate imbalance of *vata doshas*. In these two imbalances, it is easy for the Ayurveda doctor to treat.

One Mr. Annaiah, a contractor, was a chronic alcoholic. He was put on Ayurveda medicine with meditation. He abstained from alcohol, but his original symptoms of shaking hand, head, anxiety with severe sleeplessness continued with abstinence.

In order to stabilise the chemically imbalanced *vata*, it is very necessary to adhere to meditation. The normal rhythm of *vata* will be restored by this simple technique.

How to stop smoking

Ayurveda has advocated medicated smoking in *kapha* disorders, but it has not advocated ordinary smoking with nicotine content of tobacco. Nicotine is a habit forming drug, hence, it cannot be withdrawn all of a sudden. The best way is to withdraw it gradually. This has to be done along with meditation. It influences the quantum mechanical body to refrain from smoking. One must distract one's mind to other activities that is to say you must be engaged or else the *vata* will take upper hand and create a lot of addictive signs and symptoms.

Cigarette smoking has to be gradually withdrawn along with meditation or else it will be difficult for the addicted person to leave it easily, as nicotine is a dangerous habit forming drug. If you are smoking 10 cigars per day, then you have to reduce it to 8, 7, 6, 5, 4, 3, 2, 1, and stop. This is like withdrawing of cortisone with tapering its dose. Stopping the cigar will create a lot of side effects. The following procedures are necessary to stop smoking:

1. Start meditation.
2. Cleanse the system with detoxifying method as *panchakarma* therapy.
3. Regular Ayurvedic yoga exercises.
4. Balanced breathing.

5. Adhere to constitutional type of foods. Usually *vata* pacifying diets are good.
6. Oil to pacify *vata*.
7. Medicated anti-*vata* treatment of enema.

The patient must take proper guidance from an ayurvedic doctor about the nature of his constitution, type of food, and the ways of taking medicated enemas. For *vata*, in order to get it balanced at the earliest, is to take medicated decoction enema alternated with oily enemas. The schedule of enemas are 8, 6, and 30 *yoga, kala* and *karmavasti* respectively. Any one of these schedules can be tried, depending upon the nature and severity of the condition of the diseases and the constitution of the person. One must know that *vata* alleviating diet is equally important for getting good and early relief.

One has to come to a normal day-to-day work, as soon as his tension of smoking withdrawn gradually. The patient must have a courage to take this treatment. If one schedule of treatment brings him relief, then he has to continue it till he gets good appetite, sleep and happiness in body and pleasantness in the mind. It may be noted here that all the signs and symptoms of earlier smoking will completely disappear.

The *panchakarama* therapy is a widely accepted treatment for cleansing and detoxifying the body, in order to bring back the aggravated *dosha* to their balanced state. One must also take some tonics for the upliftment of nervous system. Some of the ayurvedic drugs like Ashwagandha and its preparation will soothen the body and invigorate the nervous system.

How safe is smoking—recent views: How to stop smoking

It is not analytic that nicotine will depress the brain cells and make a person smoke more and more. Nicotine is absorbed through nose and mouth. One puff of cigarette consists of 4000 toxic chemicals including nicotine. It is rapidly absorbed in the system. Smoking produces reproductive health problems and reproductive hazards in the person:

In man.

1. Potency of sex diseases
2. Fertility is impaired
3. Movement of sperms decreases
4. Sperms count will be reduced
5. Abnormal sperms will be increased.

In female

1. Egg production of ovum will be decreased.
2. Premature/preterm labour will increase.
3. Implantation of ovum will fail.
4. Abortion is very common.

Nicotine has cancer production chemicals. Nicotine is an addictive drug like pethidine.

Chapter Nine

PREMATURE AGEING IS PREVENTABLE

Man is microcosm of the universe. The world is made up of *pancha mahabhutas*, earth, air, water, fire and ether. The body is also made up of the above *pancha mahabhutas* in different proportions. These pancha mahabhutas go into formation of three *doshas* and seven *dhatus* etc.

Consuming coffee or tea, early in the morning, especially before brushing the teeth is not good for health.

Can ageing be prolonged

Age is controlled by food habits, sleep and sexual behaviours.

Tips for prolonging life

If one wants to live long at least one hundred years, one must follow the following things without fail.

1. Get up in the morning at 4:30 a.m. and wash your face and mouth. Brush your teeth and clean your tongue.
2. Do your Ayurvedic exercises.
3. Do *pranayama* (balanced breathing) regularly which controls your mind and body and will not allow you to forget your daily programmes.
4. *Pargnyaparadha* is the word used for forgetting and doing unholy and wrong deeds, avoid it.
5. Have oil bath with til oil (sesame oil) with mild massage, as heavy massage aggravates *vata*.

6. Put ear drops in your ears.
7. Put errhine (nasal drops) with Anutaila.
8. Take bath with warm water to body and lukewarm water to head.
9. Meditation 15-20 minutes.
10. Take breakfast between 6-8 a.m.
11. Have lunch before 2 p.m. Drink water only after meals.
12. Take a medium or light walk after lunch.
13. Do not strain too much in your work.
14. Have evening meals between 6-8 p.m.
15. Have ¾ of stomach full food and ¼ empty.
16. Go to bed before 10 p.m.
17. Sleeping is as important as food. Good sleep promotes life.
18. Do not drink coffee, tea, alcohol, don't smoke.
19. Do not do any harm to others either physically or morally.
20. Wish others well.
21. Do not hate your enemies.
22. Sex is equally important for a prolonged life. Have coitus as per schedule. Too much of coitus will lead to many diseases and shorten your life.
23. Take daily Ayurvedic rejuvenative diets milk, ghee, Aswangandha, Chyavanaprasha *lehya*. These things tone up the muscles tissues and prolong life.
24. Eat raw vegetables daily.
25. Avoid non-vegetarian diet as it produces fats, robustness, high blood pressure and diabetes. If you cannot stop it, minimise it. Use less fat and use natural proteins and carbohydrates in *dal* and rice.
26. Do meditation early in the morning and evening for 15-20 minutes which keeps your mechanical body in peace.
27. Tell the truth and love the world.
28. Love your people and others.
29. Try to be happy, healthy and wise.

Ageing brings wear and tear

All the cells of the body are liable to wear and tear. The liver is a chemical and metabolic factory. It produces many items and destroys many. It is the seat of liver glycogen which is mobilised, when it is necessary in the muscles. Muscles glycogen on demand in the blood will be mobilised into glucose. In old age, wrinkles are seen on the skin. Muscles are wasted and appetite will be reduced, and there is less sleep. His vision becomes dull. He will be deaf and there is high blood pressure due to arteriosclerosis.

In the younger age group the cells are very active, fresh and full of vigour. But in old age, the cells will be old, with loss of vigour, passive and the tissues will be fibrous in nature. But intelligence is still sharp. The quantum mechanical body must be balanced. This is possible by meditation. The mind sends messages to all the cells of the body and stimulates and invigorates into energy and new cells will be formed in the body.

The cells are renewed and regenerated daily. This goes on in a healthy individual. It is observed in the people, who are regularly doing Ayurvedic exercises and meditation look young and also live long. If people undertake *kayakalpa* treatment, even the old people can become young like Chyavan Saint, who became young after this treatment.

Scientific evaluation of old age

The brain is the king of nerves. Brain cells are made up of neurons. These cells do not split as other cells in the body. So their number is naturally diminished. Everyday thousands of neurons die and are not replaced. But we do not feel their deficiency. The degeneration causes the weakness in brain cells and other organs and symptoms and signs of old age creep in. The defect in eyesight, deafness, loss of taste, loss of smell and loss of memory, weakness in walking, are mainly due to weakness in the cells of the brain. The kidney and other organs also considerably become weak.

The cell necrosis could be prevented by using vitamin C in large quantity. The cells will have oxidants produced from the death of the cells. These reduce the age of a person. These things can be stopped or avoided by using *amalaki* (goose berry). This is equal to a reducing agent. If one eats orange of 60 mg (with Vitamin C in it) will reduce the blood fibrinogen to 0.15 gms/l. This reduces 10% of heart attacks in an individual. So one must eat orange, lemon, karande (berry) and perale daily. The use of garlic is found to be very effective in reducing blood clotting and keeps the blood vessels in balanced state. The use of onion in the diet also has the same effect as garlic. The effects of garlic and orange are similar to heparin and warperin, which prevents clotting of the blood. These Indian drugs (herbs) have permanent and sustaining actions in preventing clotting mechanism and maintaining normal blood vessels. Thereby the heart attacks get reduced and the person lives long with perfect health.

Heredity

The adaptive capacity of a person faces weakness after a disease. This depends on the resistance power of a person called immunity. The genes DNA also have their say in promoting old age.

Immunity

In our body bone marrow, thymus, milk secreting duct, gulma (fantum tumour) secrete T-cells and B-cells ampocyte disease resistance factors. These kill the disease producing organisms and produce health in an individual.

In old age, the immunity will become weak and subsequently it promotes old age. They are more prone to diseases. They may not live more than ninety years.

The following factors will reduce the resistance of the body and come in the way of prolonging life.

1. Air
2. Water
3. Food

Air

Air is essential for our living. Most of the trees, shrubs take carbondioxide for their growth and leave oxygen to nature. Man inspires oxygen and expires carbondioxide. Factories creates health hazard leading to cold and respiratory allergies, cough, tuberculosis, cancer of the lungs, skin allergies and other respiratory disorders in the body leading to disorders at the quantum level of the body and mind. Man requires oxygen for the growth of the body and for his living. The ozone layer of the nature is also essential for the well-being of the human beings. This is also being damaged due to excessive pollution, that takes place every day in this world. The best thing would be to grow more trees like neem and also to prevent air pollution through different advanced scientific techniques.

Water

Water is necessary for our body functions and growth. Even in olden days, purified water was being supplied to people. Our body consists of 80-90% water. This should be pure and pleasant to body and mind. To prepare foods—in cleaning of utensils, in cooking and also to take bath and to grow plants, water is a dire necessity.

Pollution of water takes place from the sewage and factories effluent. The treatment of polluted water and sewage water will to some extent prevent diseases. Underground drainage also pollutes the water supply to the public. Hence, this type of water supply will be unfit for human consumption. In olden days they use to purify the water–as *kathaka* seeds (Strychnos Potatorum) are put to water and preserved for a day or two will purify the water. Another method of purification of water is of three pots method which was in vogue in ancient India. In addition to the above the purification of water by chlorine and other chemicals are an added advantage to purify the excessive pollution of water.

Food

Food is also equaly important for the well-being of man. The vegetables, cereals, corn, wheat, ragi, rice, and other leafy vegetables are good for health. Some people who are accustomed to non-vegetarian diet, can also take less fat with a minimum quantity as excessive quantity results in many diseases.

Adulteration of food has become the order of the day. Food is grown by using chemical fertilizers. Crops are being sprayed with dangerous, poisonous chemical pesticides. DDT and other disinfectants are sprayed on the grains, corns, seeds and other food stuffs to prevent any infection. In poultry farming, poultry foods with antibiotics like tetracycline are used. Even at the quantum level of mind and body, man has become polluted. This comes in the way of reaching perfect health. The best remedy would be to grow food traditionally and also to use natural disinfectants like neem and to revive good health to live long.

Oxidants will act as an agent for adding oxygen or subtracting hydrogen from the living cells of the body. These oxidants are released from the body, whenever there is an accident and try to kill the living cells. These can be removed from the body by using reducing agents.

This is a new medicine called Orthomolecular medicine which is in the offing. Our food also contains vitamin C and vitamin E. Vitamin C prevents cancer and heart attacks. Vitamin C is present in goose berry, lemon, tamarind and other sour foods. Tulsi is also found useful in preventing heart attacks and research is going on this topic. Daily use of chyavanaprash in the diet will definitely increases age as it acts against the oxidants, which has been proved scientifically.

The application of oil to the body as *abhyanga* was advocated by Ayurveda, as it not only increases age of the person but also relieves fatigue and increases eye sight and so on. Urbanites are reluctant to get oil applied to the body. People in the west are injecting medicine through the skin. This is called transthermal therapeutic system. So, they are now reaching to 5000 years old Ayurveda method of applying oil to the body. This smoothens the body nerves, increases circulation to the cells of the body as well as other organs.

The role of free radicals in enhancing age

Oxygen is essential for our living. But at times it is dangerous to our life. To quote an example, oxygen is necessary to produce Adenosine phosphate from the cells after its spilt with glucose. Then, during process oxygen will be converted as free radicals. The atom is converted externally with electron. These free radicals react with cells and remove its minute parts. The free radicals will cause daily irreparable damage to the cells and cause old age. The antioxidants play a major role in preventing old age. These are present in vitamin C, A, E which are already explained. These are present in our food. Ayurveda has advocated the use of Rasayana (chyavanaprasha, ashwagandha leha), the tissues builder with vitamin A, C, and E to promote long life. Even in this so-called advanced scientific age, the 5000 years old Ayurveda and its doctrines have a say in promoting long life by rejuvenating brain and other cells of the body.

Rasayana for longer life (eriatrics)—A boon to old age

Ayurveda science consists of thousands of herbs. We use them either in cooking or in the form of juices to quench thirst. Some of the drugs stimulate the liver cells. Some of the drugs promote eye sight.

The pungent drugs act as *antikapha* and remove the phlegm or mucus. *Mahasudarshana churna* is bitter and it acts on *pitta* and reduces *pitta* and its aggravation like fever.

Ayurveda advocates the use of whole plant rather than the active ingredients. Modern medicine uses active ingredients of the drug which produces complications.

There is a likelihood of adverse effects. The whole plant if used will not create any complications, as there will be some antagonistic drugs in itself.

How Rasayana drugs work

Ayurveda, the science of life, pleads that everything, every plant, metal, minerals in this world, if used with care and caution, according to their property, act as food, some as medicine-cum-food. Some drugs are stimulating, invigorating and some for pacifying the *doshas* as *vata*, *pitta* and *kapha*. Some drugs are liver stimulating and few drugs are diaphoretic and some are tranquilisers as *brahmi* (gotukola). Some are brain tonics, liver and spleen tonics. Some are used in urinary complaints as *gokshura* (tribulus terristris). So the use of drugs or herbs runs into a compendium. Our Ayurvedic saints have written their properties of taste as sweet, pungent, astringent, salt, bitter and sour, and cold and hot potency. Their use is as either tonics or as against doshas. Some drugs are for emaciation and some drugs for obesity and so on. Some drugs for *doshas* for *vata*-madhuyasti (licorice), for *pitta*-

figs, saffron, for *kapha*-honey. These drugs are magico spiritual in nature.

Nature of plants

Every member of every species will have distinct features. Specific herbs are used for a specific purpose and these should be taken under the guidance of an Ayurvedic doctor. Every gem stones, colours, tastes aromas are used as medicines in addition to foods. Every herb is selective in its action. Each herb acts on the cell. They have cell affinity. The cell is also made up of *panchabhautic*. So also the herbs. Some drugs are also specific in their action. To quote an example the *gokushara* acts on the kidneys. Bitter drugs on liver, *aswagandha* on nerves and *brahmi* (*gotakola*) on brain. *Rasayana* herbs are the speciality of Ayurveda. No such explanations are found elsewhere. Some of the drugs stimulate insulin productions and thyroxine growth hormone and anti-diuretic hormone. In India, these are used as medicine but in foreign countries, they are not recognised as medicine, but as food supplements.

The Amalki (Indian gooseberry) contains five tastes. In addition to the tastes it has got plenty of vitamins C, but according to Ayurveda it acts as powerful rejuvenator of cells of the body. It tones up the system by stimulating the sluggish and lethargic cells to active action. It rejuvenates lungs, heart, liver and blood including reproductive organs and endocrine glands.

Rasayana tonic cum medicine

The herbs which are used daily along with food are not only toning up the cells of the body, but also one herb will act as only one type of cells. The *brahmi* (*gotukola*) acts only on brain cells and nerve cells. The *aswagandha* (withania somnifera) acts on nerve cells. So it is a nerve tonic and it acts on the reproduction cell of the male. It is a sex tonic. Garlic which is used in our daily preparation is a powerful anticholesterol drug. It also prevents clotting. So, it is a safe drug to be used to prevent heart attacks. The *commiphora mukul guggulu* is also widely used as an anti-obesity, it is gum of a plant grown in Gujarat state. These *rasayanas* are potent life promoters, life saving herbs, which rejuvenate the body and mind tissues at the quantum level. The health of the person will be restored to normal and the longevity of the individual will be attained. So, one can live long with these Rasayanas, which are harmless herbs but, yet safe without any side effects. The chyavanaprash a linctus, *bramha rasayana, ashwagandha rasayana* are some of the few important tonics which are commonly used in India. These *rasayanas* will help to stop the degeneration in the cells of the body and mind and produce regeneration in the cells. That is the ultimate aim of the Ayurveda to live in good and perfect health for long period.

The *gotakola* improves the speech in children who stammer. It increases the concentration and intellectual capacity in students. It promotes sharp decision making skills in housewives and executives. It revitalises the nerve cells and brain cells by simulating and invigorating brain cells. It aids in expanding the understanding and makes one more intelligent. It improves concentration, memory and sharpness of mental and physical reflexes. So to say, it is tonic to the brain without any side effects.

Benefits of rasayana therapy

1. These *rasayanas* are either working as a tonic to the body or as specific for some malady.
2. These *rasayanas* are potent life promoters, life saving herbs which rejuvenate the cells and body tissues.
3. The health of the person will be restored and the longevity of the individual attained.
4. One can live long with these *rasayanas* which are harmless herbs but safe without any side effects.

5. The *chyavanaprasha linctus, bramah rasayana, aswagandha rasayana* are some of the important tonics which are commonly used.

6. All the herbs of Ayurveda are either medicine when they are taken or work as a tonic to the body and rejuvenate the system. These will help to stop degeneration in the cells of the body. The regeneration in the cells is the ultimate aim of Ayurveda.

7. Ayurveda's main aim is to attain good health and to live long.

How to assess your age

The way to live longer with Ayurveda style of living, diurnal regimen, seasonal regimen. Ayurvedic exercise, meditation, *panchakarma* therapy and so on. With these things one can live minimum hundred years. Each 12 points taken for excellent, 6 points for average, 0 points for below Average. You can arrive at a final number after you follow health schedule for six months and once again see the difference.

1. Happiness

very happy	12	points
good	6	points
similar to others	0	points

2. Job Bsatisfaction

When start going to work

Interested in new work	12	points
Courage to do the work	6	points
No interest in work	0	points

3. Cholesterol

The rate of cholesterol

Good-180mg	12	points

Minimum-200mg   6   points
Very poor-250mg   0   points

4. Blood pressure

130/90 above 40 years Good	12	points
130/90 above minimum	6	points
140/90 or more poor	0	points

5. Heart attack

Before 50 to 60 years—Not even one	12	points
One or two or three	6	points
6 or more	0	points

6. Physical examination

This includes the colour of the skin, tongue coated or not. Vision is good or not, weakness, respiration, and physical fatigue etc.

It is same daily	12	points
Little changes	6	points
Suffering from disease	0	points

7. Alcohol addiction

Never taken alcohol	12	points
Occasional	6	points
Drinking everyday	0	points

8. Smoking of cigarettes

Never smoke	12	points
Occasionally	6	points
Smoking daily	0	points

9. Health

This belongs to physical mental and spiritual health.

Good	12	points
Medium health	6	points
Poor	0	points

10. General intellect

Good	12	points
Medium	6	points
Poor	0	points

11. Memory

Whether one has less memory or nil

Excellent	12	points
Good	6	points
Poor	0	points

Make final score.

Rasayana

Recent studies on *rasayana* have shown that it reduces clotting of blood and acts as prophylactic for cancer. It prevents free radicals which in turn initiate the prolonging of life.

Undergoing the *panchkarma* therapy at least once in 6 months or a year will make the body young by 5-6 years. Meditation done after *panchkarma* therapy will be more beneficial than meditation itself. Mr. V.V.Giri, former President of India, had undergone *panchakarma* therapy for a month.

In order to prevent premature ageing one has to adopt a diet according to one's constitution, daily routine, seasonal routine, Ayurvedic exercise, *panchakarma* with meditation with *rasayanas* preparations or with all these things one can live at least one hundred years with a hale and healthy body and pleasantness of mind.

Part C
Try to Live with Nature

Chapter Ten

IMPELLING FORCE TO DEVELOP

The word "try to live with nature" is the fundamental belief of Ayurveda.

We live, breath, eat and sleep—all are part of nature. The desire of the body is sent through the quantum level to the mind and to the body. Crores of impulses are being transmitted to mind from the body. There are 50 trillion cells in the body and each of these cells transmits messages to centres in the hypothalamus, which connects mind and body. So this neuro transmitter will make one act. This must start at the quantum body. The mind and body link will be made in the brain. The man will be happy as long as he is satisfied with his desire. To quote an example, if Mr. Sagar needs sweet foods, then he will feel satisfied. This is being done from the taste buds present in the tongue, which send messages to brain centre in the hypothalamus. Then the mind says it is sweet and thereby happiness results.

In case, the pathway is interfered, then one can conclude that we are not in tune with nature.

Suppose one is in a balanced state of mind and body but eats voraciously, it will lead to bad health. As a result, indigestion will lead to many diseases. In the forthcoming chapters, I have tried to give readers, the variety of food, daily routines, seasonal routine and exercise which are all in tune with nature, as per Ayurveda.

How to make best and right choices

As one starts progressing and tries to live with nature, one will make the best choice out of the right things. This will occur in a day, hour to hour or minute to seconds. These things go on endlessly. So, it is not easy to stop in correct choices. Whatever choice you make, finally the quantum body will decide what is right and what is wrong. The internal conflict between the external likes and mind may differ leading to ill-health.

If both are in tune with body and mind, then it is balanced state called perfect health. Mr. Verghese is an obese person who eats food recklessly, in spite of warnings of the physicians, and undergoes several treatments, consults physicians, psychiatrists, psychologists and surgeons without any benefit for his obesity.

Ayurveda advocates that such a person should limit his desire of eating to minimum. It can be possible only, when he becomes *satvic*. There are three impulses as *satva*, *rajas*, and *tamas*.

The *satva* will have calmness, tolerance, bravery, firmness, equality of mind, faith in God, contentment, quickness and adaptability. But the *rajas* and *tamas* will have lust, anger, fear, doubtfulness of mind, desires, talkative, worry and lethargy.

If Mr. Verghese wants to attain good health from obesity, he should start meditation. He must go towards *satva* to progress or stay in the same *rajas* or *tamas* and suffer.

Ayurveda pleads that one must attain *satvic* to be more healthy and creative in life. *Satvic* people will be naturally healthy. When *satvic* property is lacking in the brain, then the impurity starts in the activities of man. Ayurveda gives the reason for such an imbalance in the mind as lethargy, mental inertia, fear, doubtful mind, desires, anger, violent behaviour or reading books related to violence.

Psychological causes

Stress and strain, loss of memory, death of the nearest and dearest, living in unwholesome surroundings and intake of unwholesome diet, negative thinking, emotion, fear, greediness and discontentment also lead to defect in satva guna.

On seeing violence in films, our mind develops an unhealthy atmosphere triggered in the brain, which causes obstruction in *manovahasrotas* impulses transmitting nerves and creates different types of activities, which are dangerous to health.

This, coupled with various addictions leads to blockage at some level of the body and the mind and disturbs the balance of the *doshas* triggering a disease. In order to correct it several remedies will be explained to readers. *Panchakarm*a therapies, daily routine, seasonal routine, proper diet, meditation, bliss therapy, music therapy, and so on. With all these things the imbalanced state of the mind will be brought to a state of *satvic* in nature, which will promote perfect health in an individual. *Satva* teaches us how to live with others, how to respect others, how to respect elders, teachers and how to take food. So, it is *satva* which is the natures part and act always in terms of balancing the body. So to live in tune with nature is aptly and rightly said in our texts of Ayurveda.

How to promote satva in human beings

Ayurveda recommends some important things to promote *satva* quality in our body and mind. Eating unadulterated food, drinking pure water, inhaling pure air and getting good sleep at night and rest—all these are necessary to keep the mind in tranquility. At the same time, one has to visit beautiful gardens, lakes, streams, rivers, hills and mountains, trees, sound of birds and animals. These are all part of nature, which make one's senses pleased and purify them. Ayurveda is the *upaveda* of *Atharavana veda*. For promoting *satva* qualities in man, they have recommended certain factors:

1. Be generous to others—treat each one of them alike with dignity and respect.
2. Be pleasant and good to others.
3. Avoid anger and criticism.
4. Move with good people.
5. Spend your days in good company, for playing and relaxation and for spending time.
6. Eat three-fourths of your hunger or capacity.
7. Awake early in the morning in *brahma muhurtha* (4:30–6:00 a.m.), walk in good climate for at least 2-3 kilometers. It helps you to get good oxygen and ozone to body and also is a good exercise.
8. Try to follow the rules of balance in talk, speech, sleep, and food.
9. Try to be tolerant to others.
10. Try to love animals.
11. Treat everybody with love and affection.
12. Try to love nature.
13. For an intelligent person, everything is good in this world and for a fool, everything is bad and useless.
14. Eat natural foods, vegetables, milk, rice, ragi, ghee and wheat, a list of *sativic* food is given in this book.

With all these things the nature will fulfil your needs and necessities. *Satvic* man lives happily, healthily and he becomes a model to others. That is the nature's gift to man.

Chapter Eleven

DIURNAL ROUTINE: DINACHARYA
OBEYING RULES OF NATURE

A **Daily Routine** is nature's boon to protect and to preserve health. Ayurveda lays special emphasis on the prevention of diseases and protection of health. The health as defined in Ayurveda is the balanced equilibrium of doshas, digestive fire, tissues and toxins or *malas* of the body and pleasantness of mind. This is similar to the W.H.O definition of health. In order to achieve this healthy goal, one has to adopt and practise certain principles with regard to diet, behaviour, conduct, habit and seasons. These principles are known as *charyas* or routine lifestyle of an individual.

Now we consider daily routine

A natural life is regulated according to one's constitution or *prakriti*. It is essential to say that one must follow a daily regimen, since the dawn of the day to the time he goes to bed.

The mysteries of nature includes man, his body and mind. Man is composed of the senses body, mind and *atma* (soul). The food that we take will be converted into necessary things for the blood, nerves, mind and intellect. In our body, the heart beats 72 times per minute and the respiratory rate ranges from 14-15 per minute. The food that we take goes into metabolic changes to fit into several types of tissues. Bone, muscle, cartilage, tendon, hairs, skin, stomach, bladder and uterus are made up of smooth muscles and eyes and so on. It is a complicated mechanical body that one cannot manufacture in the laboratory easily.

In the morning one takes breakfast, then one gets a little sluggish and lazy due to *kapha*. The body will be a little cold in the morning. In the *pitta* period 10 am to 2 p.m. the body will become warm and digestive and metabolic systems will gear up to meet the challenge of food intake.

Then *vata* predominance time is from 2 p.m. to 6 p.m. It mainly controls the nervous system—both sympathetic and parasympathetic. There are three cycles as stated here.

Kapha cycle is from 6 a.m. to 10 a.m. and *pitta* cycle is from 10 a.m. to 2 p.m. and *vata* cycle is from 2 p.m. to 6 p.m. The second cycle runs as *kapha* 6 p.m. to 10 p.m. *pitta* from 10 p.m.to 2 a.m. *Vata* 2 a.m. to 6 a.m. These cycles are going to have a master control for any layman. God, the creator of universe, had made this special creation of man.

A person should wake up before 5.30 a.m. have his breakfast before 8 a.m. He should complete his lunch before 1 p.m. and dinner before 8 p.m. One must go to bed before 10 p.m. as *pitta* period will come afterawards and he may not get sleep during that period.

Tips for best ways for a healthy life

1. One must awake before 5.30 a.m. in *brahma muhurtha* or before sunrise.
2. Evacuate bladder and bowel.
3. Drink a glass of lukewarm water to facilitate easy, bowel movement, cold water for *pitta* constitution and for *vata* warm or hot water.
4. Brush the teeth with bitter sticks as *babulla*, neem etc, or Ayurvedic tooth powder/tooth paste.
5. Scrape the tongue with silver tongue cleaner or any plastic tongue cleaner.
6. Do some exercise, Ayurvedic exercise and *pranayama*-balanced breathing.

7. Have massage with til oil (sesame).
8. Take hot water bath 15 minutes after exercise or use warm water to body and lukewarm to head.
9. Do meditation preferably transcendental meditation which keeps mind in tranquility and helps the entire day's work in a smooth manner.
10. Have breakfast.
11. Take a short walk.
12. Have lunch before 1 p.m. take rest for some-time.
13. Small walk, meditation if possible.
14. Have moderate dinner at 8 p.m. and take rest for 5-10 minutes.
15. Walk a few distance.
16. Drink butter milk after dinner.
17. Light activities.
18. Go to bed early before 10 p.m. and don't read or see TV.

Cycles of doshas

I Cycle

Kapha- 6 a.m. to 10 a.m.
Pitta- 10 a.m. to 2 p.m.
Vata- 2 p.m. to 6 p.m.

II Cycle

6 p.m. to 10 p.m.
10 p.m. to 2 a.m.
2 a.m. to 6 a.m.

This is an ayurvedic schedule. One has to plan his day with the above schedule, in order to maintain a balanced health. If he does not follow this schedule he may be prone to many diseases.

Waking up between 4.30 a.m. to 6.00 a.m. in the morning time is special time in Ayurveda. As soon as he wakes up he should plan for the entire day. He should be free from worries. He must be in calm mood. The toxins of the waste products will be expelled from the body as urine and faeces.

One has to clean his teeth to prevent bad smell from the mouth. The tongue must be properly cleaned to prevent *ama* in the body resulting in improper digestion. The scraping of the tongue cleans it and also stimulates it by inceasing circulation. *Gandusha* (gargling) with til oil (sesame) will make the taste buds, purifies and stimulates the normal functions. Mix warm water ½ cup with 1 teaspoon of sesame oil and gargle for one minute. This works against *vata*, as it is oily and *vata* is dry.

Ayurvedic exercise will be dealt in the book (chapter 16). The *pranayama*, the breathing exercise is also explained in the same chapter.

How to do Abhyanga (oil massage)

Abhyanga oil massage is a speciality of ayurveda procedure. A person who wants to have oil massage must pass urine and faeces and clean his hands. He should remove clothes if necessary. He/she may cover their private parts of the body.

How to prepare the oil

The til oil (sesame oil) is available in all the leading general stores. 25 ml of the oil is taken in a cup and made warm equally to the body temperature. It should not be over heated or under heated, the oil is heated to normal body temperature. It must be applied on the body from the head to the toe without leaving any place.

Type of massage

The massage must be mild. In the joints, it should be circular. The ears must also be nourished with the oil, ear drops must be put to ears. Massage should not be harsh as it increases *vata*. It should be mild or smooth in nature as it pacifies *vata*.

Benefits of oil massage

1. It relieves fatigue.

2. It prevents ageing.
3. It relieves pains.
4. It promotes good vision.
5. It strengthens the body.
6. It gives good sleep.
7. It gives good colour and brightness to the skin.

One must not expose the body to cold climate and external atmosphere immediately after massage or during the period of the massage, to prevent a cold attack.

Lunch between 1 to 1.30 p.m.

It is a *pitta* time with enough digestive fire. So one must have lunch in time 1 to 1.30 p.m. or before 1.30 p.m. One must not eat too much. One should not drink alcohol as it depresses the system and causes lethargy at work. Ice, cold drinks, ice creams, iced fruits and salads are taboo. Drinking coffee or tea is equally bad, as these will certainly impair the digestion. Coffee contains caffeine, and tea contains tannin, both affect the body and come in the way of good health by prevenling absorption of iron in the gut leading to anaemia.

After meals, one must have 10-15 minutes of rest. Sit quietly or take a small walk. This promotes good digestion. Generally, one will not get complication, as the person getting oil massage will never be exposed, at least half an hour after bath. The body massage may take 10-15 minutes. The oil can be removed with Ayurvedic powder or soap. This oil is good for *vata* constitution but for *pitta* constitution, coconut oil can be used. Oil penetrates into the skin easily as its molecule is smaller than the rabid virus. Oil's effects on the skin as its smoothing and cooling effect are well known. One of the seats of *vata* is skin. So, the massage has got intense action on the nervous system.

Dinner between 6 to 8 p.m.

The dinner period is the *kapha* period from 6 p.m. to 10 p.m. So one has to take minimum dinner. All fermented foods are forbidden, as sour cream, yogurt and cheese which will impair the digestion as a result. *Ama* is produced which is bad for health and produces many diseases.

Drinking tea, alcohol, coffee are not advisable. However, fresh juice from raw vegetables can be taken. It is proved that raw juices will stimulate the insulin secretion in the body. Alcohol drinking is not at all good as it is highly toxic to body and habit forming. This immediately damages the liver, producing liver cirrhosis and sometimes cancer and diabetes. Those who cannot leave it are advised to drink in moderation. Spend your after dinner time till 10 p.m. with family and friends or by either reading or watching T.V. Sleeping afterwards being the *pitta* period. So, one may not get sleep. It is not at all good to see. T.V beyond 10 p.m.

Bed time

It is good to go to bed at 10 p.m. or before 10 p.m. It is a *kapha* period and you will get sleep. It may not be possible to get sleep after 10pm, as it is the *pitta* period.

SEASONAL ROUTINE: RITUCHARYA TO BALANCE THE ENTIRE YEAR

The skin is one of the important organs of the mechanical body. Heat and cold is regulated by it. More so the *doshas* as *vata* will be accentuated due to cold air, dry wind and cold climate. In summer, the hot climate accumulates *pitta*. In the spring (March and upto mid-June) the cold wet climate accumulates *kapha*. So the skin plays a prominent role in the quantum mechanical human body for upkeeping of health and its balance. Changes in the nature are likely to affect the body. So one must adopt and adjust to nature and its changes with foods and regimen.

Time moves in seconds, minutes, hours, days, weeks, months and years. The year is divided into six seasons.

Time is an important factor with regard to *doshas*, their normal balancing, their deficiency and their aggravation. There are three *doshas* in the body. *Kapha* time is morning, sunrise to 10 a.m. In this period the people feel little heavy, but energetic and fresh and active to do any work.

At mid morning the Kapha dosha merges into *pitta*, after 10 a.m. to 2 p.m. The individual gets hungery and his body becomes hot and light. From 2 p.m. to 6 p.m. is the vata period. During this period, there will be activeness and lightness in the body. From 6 p.m. to 10 p.m. it is again *kapha* period due to cold air with inertia, there will be less energy, *pitta* time is from 10 p.m. to 2 a.m. This cycle repeats. To sum up, the dry cold weather, along with cold wind aggravates and accumulates *vata* in the body.

When the temperature is humid, it aggravates *pitta* and leads to its accumulation. *Kapha*, is accumulated due to cold snow or wet weather. The word aggravation means increases and covers the near by places. This leads to increase in the series of the dosha accumulation means, it imbalances in *doshas*, whether, it is *vata* or *pitta* or *kapha*.

Seasons and doshas

The seasons plays a major role in unbalancing the *doshas*. Their accumulation and aggravation lead to disorder or disease. In order to prevent such a catastrophe, it is imperative for people to adopt measures such as diet and activities that are advocated in Ayurveda. In India, even today, it is being practised, if not all the people, majority of people are getting good health and longevity. Rhythmic changes occur in a person in a day with relevant *dosha* of the season throughout the year. Ayurveda has advocated three seasons instead of six seasons.

Vata season

It links the autumn and winter i.e. mid-October to mid-March.

Pitta season

It comes in summer and early autumn i.e. mid June to mid-October.

Kapha season

It is usually in spring i.e. mid-March to mid-June.

The daily cycle as already explained, starts with *kapha* and ends with *vata*. The wet cold weather in spring along with cold wind accumulate *kapha*. The hot weather accumulates *pitta* in summer and also in early autumn.

The wet dry cold weather as cold air/wind will accumulate *vata* in the body. The six seasons are common in India but in Germany one cannot have more than two seasons—cold season or little hot season. So also in America and other countries. It may be noted here that the external atmosphere has got an overall influence on the body, as body is a prototype of the nature. The body is composed of earth, water, fire, air and ether (*akasha*) in proper proportions. So any change that occur in the outside world will have a definite impact on the health of the person. One can easily recognise, which *dosha* is more in what season. For example, any cold damp, snow climate in a day occurs one can come to a conclusion that *kapha* is predominant that day.

How to adopt and adapt seasonal routine

In order to balance *doshas* in the body, it is good for a person to follow and to adopt the seasonal routine as stated in Ayurveda. This need not be a complete change in the schedule of food or activities, but only a minor change occurs. The details of the *doshas*, diet must be taken in consultation with an Ayurveda doctor.

Kapha season is spring and early summer. During this period the individual gets good strength. It is cold at night. The sun will be covered and its heat on the surface is gradually less. The moon will be blown to its natural shape. The Hemanta Ritu is the tail end phase of *visarga kala*. The digestive fire will be increased. So, one must consume food at a proper time and in proper quantity. One should take a diet which is less oily and light.

One must do exercise suitable to high strength. It is better to take more pungent, bitter and astringent food.

Pitta season

It is mid summer and early autumn (*varsh* and *sharad*). In this period, the digestive fire will be decreased due to

cloudiness in the atmosphere. The sun's rays are covered
and semidarkness prevails with drizzling. The earth is
hot and humid. Therefore, *pitta* aggravation takes place
and later on other *doshas* will be simultaneously vitiated.
The mild laxatives or purgatives as *triphala/senna* leaves
or castor oil must be taken once in a week. Food consists
of meat soup reared in dry lands. It must be taken along
with rice. Horse grams, bengal gram, *tuvardhal* soup any
one can be taken by vegetarian people. Curd with rock
salt or *panchakola* powder must be used for drinking. Less
sour, salt, ghee and oils shall be used in the diet. Light
diet is the rule. Honey must be used in minimum quantity
to pacify any *kapha* aggravation. So one should take food
and drinks that are cooling in nature, Ice cold food are
tabooed. More fluids are needed to quench thirst. Use
more of sweet, bitter and astringent tastes.

Doshas and seasonal variations

Dosha	Sanchaya	Prakopa	Prasama
Vata	Grishma	Varsha	Sharad
Pitta	Varsha	Sharad	Hemantha
Kapha	Sisira	Vasantha	Grishma

Seasons

	Food	Activities and Purification	
Hemantha	Nutritious	Massage	
Sishira	Sweet	Exercise	
	Sour	Woolen blankets/protection	
	Salt	Against cold	
Vasantha	light	Massage	Vomiting therapy

contd...

	Dry Laja and Chanka	Exercise	Fomentation therapy
Grishma	Sweet Light Oily Light In digestion Seasonal Fruits, Mango, Jamoon	cold air ushira	
Varsha	Astringent Sweat, salt, light Diet, boiled and clean Curd, lemon		Avoid sleeping Dirty water is cleaned by monsoon
Shardritu	Sweat Astringent Oily food Specially Milk Ghee, sweets Rice	to sit in monlight in first quarter of night exercise, Avoid curd	purgat or Blood letting

Vata season
(Late autumn and early winter)

It is in this season that more of oily foods, heavy and warm diet, warm and drinks are advisable. This is done to pacify *vata*, food with sweet, sour and salt tastes are good. The digestive fire requires heavy and oily food for its maintenance.

Some useful hints
1. Eat fresh and warm foods.
2. Eat locally grown food as they are amenable to our health.

3. *Pitta* summer, *vata* winter, *kapha* spring, adjust your diet and activities.
4. The role of *parkriti* and balanced food; *Vata* pacifying diet in winter, *kapha* pacifying diet in spring, *pitta* pacifying diet in summer.
5. If two *doshas* are in excess then mix foods half and half of each *dosha* and take.
6. If one does not adhere to the rules of the diet and activities of each season, naturally it leads to many undesirable complications in the body and it leads to diseases and unhealthiness, so one should avoid and adopt procedures stated above for promotion and preservation of good health.
7. Early to bed and early to rise makes you healthy, wealthy and wise. And it is good to remember, good health, good character and normal values are the real assets in life. Avoid or reduce fried and refried foods, high protein, fat, salt and sugar, sour and gas forming food.
8. Take a well-balanced wholesome food high in fibre, less fat and proteins eat at fixed hours. Drink at least 3 litres of water, have sound sleep at night, and relax after continuous work for a healthy living.

Uttarayana and Dakshanayana

In uttarayana sun is rising to Northern Hemisphere. The sun is very hot and it dries up the oilness of the earth, which results in weakness and general debility in man. In dakshanayana the sun rises to Southern Hemisphere and produces cloudiness, gales with continuous rain which cools the hot atmosphere. Human beings restore their normal strength. The moon is more in this period. In *varsha Ritu* minimum uctuaresness will be present with sour taste in foods. Sharad Ritu gives medium strength to body and salty tastes in foods. In Hemanta Ritu moon becomes more and sun recedes there will be sweet taste in foods and

Uttarayana and Dakshanayana

more strength in the body. The strength will be less in summer and rainy season. The strength will be more in cold and winter season. In Sisira Ritu, the *vayu* and *akasa* will be in predominance in nature with bitter taste (*vayu* and *akasha*). Vasanta Ritu consists of more of *vayu* and *prithvi* in nature of astringent taste (*vayu* and *prithvi*) in the body.

In Greeshma Ritu vayu and tejas will be more in nature with pungent taste (*vayu + tejas*). Varsha Ritu consists of *prithvi* and *tejo bhutas* in the nature in predominance with sour taste (*prithvi + tejas*). In Sharad Ritu, *jala* and *telobhutas* will be more in nature with salty taste (*jala + teja*). Hemanta Ritu consists of more of *prithvi* and *jala mahabhutes* in nature, with more of sweet taste (*prthvi + jala bhutas*)

So, one has to adjust the food regimen according to season to balance the imbalanced *doshas* to attain good health leading to perfect health.

SISHIRA RITU: Late winter (February, March)

Foods good for the people in this season:

Vegetables: Bottlegourd, cabbage, greygourd, lady's finger, pumpkin, and tomato.
Cereals: New rice, new millet and wheat.
Podgrains: Black gram and green gram.
Tubers and roots: Beetroot, carrot, ginger, potato
Meat: Chicken, fish, mutton and prawns.
Fruits: Apple, copra, grapes, orange and pineapple.
Milk: Butter, cheese, buttermilk, cream, ghee and milk.
Other foods: Cashewnut, pista, sesame, sugar and sweets
Water: Lukewarm.

Foods not good for the people

Vegetables: Bittergourd, brinjal, dried, fenugreek, drumstick and sunflower.
Cereals: Barley, old millet and old barley.
Grains: Beans, dry grain lentil, and peas.
Meat: Crabs, fried and dried meat.
Tubers and roots: Garlic, lotus-root and radish.
Fruits: Jamboo.
Other foods: Cumin seeds, fried foods, mustard and red chillies.
Water: Cold water.

VASANTA RITU

Foods good for the people in this season: (April, May)

Vegetable: Brinjal, bittergourd, drumstick, fenugreek, amaranth and spinch.
Cereals: Barley, millet, old rice and wheat.
Grains: Gram, green grain, horse gram and yellow gram.
Tubers and roots: Carrot, garlic, onion, radish and turmeric.
Fruits: Kola, papaya and white pumpkin.

Milk products: Buttermilk.
Meat: Crabs, chicken, dried fish, fried fish, kabab, prawns, small fish and tandoori.
Other foods: Coriander seeds, cumin, asofoedita, honey, omum seeds and pepper.
Water: Ginger water, sandle + water + honey.

Foods not good for the people in this season

Vegetable: Lady's finger.
Cereals: New cereals and new rice.
Grains: Black gram and gourd.
Tubers roots: Gourd, lotus root, topioca, sago and yam.
Fruits: Apple, beetroot, cashewnut, cucumber, custard, orange, pista, peach and strawberry and plantain.
Meat: Big fish.
Milk: Cream, cheese, cowsmilk, guava and khova.
Water: Cold water and sweets.

GREESHMA RITU: (summer) (June/July)

Foods good for the people in this season

Vegetables: Bottlegourd, cauliflower, lady's finger and parwal.
Cereals: Half boiled rice, new rice and red rice.
Grains: Black and green grams and yellow grain.
Tubers roots: Beetroot, colucasia, potato, sago and yam.
Fruits: Apple, banana, custard, cucumber, dry coconut, grapes, kola, sweet orange.
Meat: Chicken, and meat.
Milk: Butter, cream, curd, ghee and milk.
Water: Camphor water, khas and rose water.

Foods not good for the people

Vegetables: Brinjal, bittergourd, drumstick, fenugreek and shimla chitti.

Cereals: Barley and maize.
Grains: Beans and horse grain.
Tubers/roots: Garlic and onion.
Fruits: Garlic and onion.
Meat: Dried mutton, fried mutton and fish.
Milk: Buttermilk and cold beverages.
Water: Cold water.

VARSHA (Monsoon) (August and September)

Food good for people in this season

Vegetables: Brinjal, bootlegourd, lady's finger and parwal.
Cereals: Half boiled rice, millet, roasted grains and wheat.
Grains: Black gram, green gram and horse gram.
Tubers/roots: Garlic, ginger, onion and yam.
Meat: Chicken and mutton.
Fruits: Dried coconut, grapes, lemon and mango.
Milk: Curd, butter milk, ghee and milk.
Others: Asafoetida, coriander, cumin, jaggery, pepper and rocksalt.
Water: Hot water.

Food not good for people

Vegetables: Bittergourd, cabbage, dried vegetables and spinach.
Cereals: Barley, maize and pearl millet.
Podgrains: Dry gram, field bean, lentil and red gram.
Tubers and roots: Carrot, chestnust, coloeasia, lotus root, sago, potato and water.
Fruits: Cucumber, jambo, melon and musk.
Meat: Dried mutton and fish.
Milk: Buffalo milk, cheese, jilebi, horse pea and sweets.
Other foods: Fried foods, sherbath and squashes.
Water: Cold water and unboiled water.

SHARAD RITU Foods advised: (October/November)

Vegetables: Amaranth, bottle gourd and bittergourd, cabbage, fenugreek, lady's finger and spinach.
Cereals: Rice, red salt, millet and wheat.
Grains: Field bean, green gram and pea.
Tubers/roots: Lotus roots, potato, sweet potato, sago, waterchestnut and yam.
Fruits: Apple, banana, fig, gooseberry granate, grapes, jambu, pomegranate, sapota and sugarcane.
Meat: Chicken and mutton.
Milk: Butter, ghee, khova, ice-cream and milk.
Other foods: Coriander seeds and leaves, honey, old jaggery,
Water: Cold water, khas water and pitcher water.

Foods to be avoided

Vegetables: Dried vegtables and drumstick.
Cereals: Maize.
Grains: Black gram, horse gram and red gram.
Meat: Crab, big fishes, dried fishes and prawns.
Fruits: Cherry, lemon, peach, pineapple, raw mango, stawberry and sour mango.
Milk: Buttermilk, curd, curry of buttermilk and gramflour.
Other foods: Asafoetida, chillies, garm masalas, mint, pepper, pickle, and sunflower oil.
Water: Lukewarm water and water preserved at night.

HEMANTA-RITU: (December-January)

Good food for in this season.

Vegetable: Bottlegourd, cabbage, fenugreek, greygourd, lady's finger, pumpkin and spinach.
Cereals: Rice, maize and wheat.
Grains (Pod): Amaranth, black gram and green gram.

Tubers and roots: Beetroot, carrot, ginger, lotusroot, onion, sweet potato.
Meat: Chicken, fish, mutton and prawns.
Fruits: Apple, banana, grapes, orange, pineapple, sapota and walnuts.
Milk: Butter, buttermilk, cheese, curd, ghee, khova and milk.
Other foods: Cloves, pista, sesame, sugar and sweets.
Water: Lukewarm.

Food not good to be taken in this season

Vegetables: Brinjal, bittergourd, dried fenugreek and drumstick.
Cereals: Barley, old cereals and millet.
Pod grains: Black gram, horse gram and red gram.
Meat: Dry meat, fried meat, small fishes.
Tubers and roots: Garlic, radish and turnip.
Fruits: Jamboo.
Other foods: Cinnamon, cumin seeds, mustard, omumwater and poppyseeds.
Water: Cold water.

In order to balance the entire year, it is necessary to follow these food charts.

Chapter Thirteen

EATING FOOD FOR PERFECT BALANCE

TYPES OF BODY

Ayurveda has postulated and practised balanced diet. It is not in the process of protein, carbohydrates and fat. It does not recommend either vitamins, minerals in terms of calories. For foreign people it is very interesting and unusual. Ayurveda nutrition depends directly on nature for insurance. Food is recommended according to *doshas*. The *doshas* consist of hot or cold, heavy or light, oily or dry and quick acting or slow acting. Ayurveda believes in *shadras* or six tastes viz sweet, bitter, astringent, sour, pungent and salty. Salty biscuits for salt, bitter gourd for bitter. Grape juice is sweet. Chillies are pungent. Neem is bitter. Amla, tamarind and lemon are sour. Ayurveda recommends food consisting of six tastes for a balanced diet in each and every meal. An Indian diet consists of sweet, rice, rasagulla, mutton fried with chillies or pepper or lemon for sour. With this, one has to understand that every meal consists of six tastes. Though some of the tastes are either more or less dependent upon the liking of the individuals.

Doshas and diet

Vata is balanced by salt, sweet and sour. *Kapha* is balanced by pungent, bitter and astringent. *Pitta* is balanced by bitter, sweet and astringent. The first taste in each dosha is powerful in balancing with *dosha*. The first taste mentioned in each *dosha* has a good effect in reducing a *dosha*.

Vata pacifying foods

The following foods are good for *vata* constitution:

1. Soothing foods like milk, cream and butter
2. Warm soups and warm foods
3. Sweet and warm foods
4. Wheat or rice
5. Tea or hot tea
6. Gotokola tea
7. Ginger tea
8. Cardamom, fennel, cinnamon
9. Warm water
10. Hot cereal
11. Warm milk at bed time
12. Til paste is best for *vata*
13. *Lassi* + cumin + ginger + salt
14. Mango pulp
15. Add *vata churna* viz. *ajamodadi churna* or *rasna churna* sprinkle on your foods at breakfast, lunch and dinner.

Foods not good for Vata

1. Dry and salty food as they are heavy
2. Seeds and nuts in small quantity
3. Unripe bananas
4. Astringent foods
5. Light and cold foods
6. Raw vegetables
7. Cold air and cold climate

Likes

Salt, sour and sweet, warm food, fat, butter and easily digestible food. *Vata* has properties of dry, cold and subtle, hence, one must take oily, hot and heavy food. In summer, we take cold drinks, cold foods which aggravate *vata*. Hence, they must be avoided. People with *vata dosha* will have bad digestion. So, one must take ginger juice with common salt or one must take butter milk with ginger or cumin powder.

The best appetiser would be ghee. The foods suggested here are to be followed by a *vata* patient, unless it is changed by an Ayurvedic physician. The vitiated *vata* causes excessive worry, hurry and other nervous symptoms and the important one is insomnia. Sweating, massaging of the body, *anuvasana* (oilenema) vasti, Niruhavasti (decoction enema) Nasya-errhine, oil drops to nose, tub-bath, *sirovasthi*, sleeping, meatsoup, ghee, blackgram, horsegram, tilseeds (sesame), *kanjee* prepared out of coriander, tender coconut water, curd, meat of animals reared in cold and marshy areas, fish, castor, green gram, brinjal, dadima (punicagranatum) gokshura, betel leaves, sugar candy, pippali, wearing of garlands of mallige flowers. Many persons with *vata* will be tired in the afternoon. It is better to take tea prepared from coriander and *aswagandha*. It is also good to take sweet and its preparations. Coffee drinking is injurious to health, as it contains caffeine, which stimulates the nervous system. Usually pungent food is not good for Vata, but chillies and spicy foods are good as they contain oil. The use of twak (cinnamon), fennel, cardamom and ginger will bring back the appetite to normal. Sweet and milk preparations are good for *vatas*. So, they must be taken whenever an individual is fatigued. It is safe to drink a soup made up of vegetables or cereals.

Generally, all sweet fruits are very good for *vata* viz mango and grapes. Apple is an astringent which requires heating before its use. It is not good for *vata*, if one takes dry food and snacks of salty origin. The oily nuts can be used to pacify *vata*, but they must be used in moderation. The best oil that can be used is til oil (seasame oil) which pacifies the Vata. Ayurveda gives due predominance to this oil as it is a powerful antidote to *vata*.

All cold, low caloried and light foods aggravate *vata*, which needs vegetables fried in oil. Salads can also be used with some oils.

Hot water is the best after a meal as it is digestive. Using cold water and ice cream are very dangerous to the body and *vata*. Hot water is digestive, diuretic and light in digestion.

Herbs and spices liked by vata people

Spices and sweets are most accepted, asafoetida, anise, basil, black pepper, cardamom, green coriander, cinnamon and clove.

Disliked by vata people

All spices must be used in minimum quantity especially astringent and bitter herbs, coriander, turmeric and fenugreek.

Nuts and seeds

Almonds are best, but all nuts and seeds must be used in moderation.

Fruits

Liked: Banana, berries, coconut, dates, figs, grapes, sweet fruits.
Disliked: Mangoes (riped), melons, oranges, papayas, pineapple, apples, pomegranate, pears (better take after boiling). All dried fruits and unriped fruits.

Vegetables

Liked: Asparagus, beets, carrots, cucumber, green beans, garlic, onion, radish, sweet potato and turnips.
Disliked: Brussels, sprouts, cabbage, cauliflower, egg plant, leafy green vegetables, raw vegetables, tomatoes, potato and peas (accepted after cooking with oil).

It is better to keep the body warm as *vata* has cold property. Warm food will be liked by *vata* person. Rice must be taken along with butter and dal. Drinking warm milk at bed time is something good to *vata* person. One should not sleep late at night, as it will cause discomfort and unhappiness in the morning.

To reduce *vata*, buttermilk is the best drink after lunch. When curd is churned and defated with equal quantity of water it is called buttermilk. It can be best taken along with cumin seeds and dry or wet ginger and common salt. Sweet mango is also good for *vata*. The *vata* pacifying *churna* like ajamodadi or Rasnadi can be added to the diet.

Vata

Grains

Liked	Disliked
Cooked oats meal	Dry oats
Wheat, rice	rice, millet

All dairy foods are acceptable to *vata* person

Meat

Liked	Disliked
Chicken and fish	usually meat, red meat

Beans

Mung beans, pink lentile, chickpeas

Oils: Sesame oil is the best oil and other oils are accepted all sweeteners are welcome.

Pitta pacifying diet

The following diets are well suited for *pitta* constitution:

1. Milk
2. Cold drinks in summer
3. Breakfast with cold cereal, apple juice
4. Grains
5. Vegetables
6. Beans
7. Salad
8. Cold water and cold foods
9. Low salt
10. Warm milk
11. Ghee—avoid if cholesterol is more.

Foods not good for Pitta

1. Pungent foods
2. Pickles
3. Sour cream and cheese
4. Coffee
5. Orange juice
6. Red Meat which produces heat
7. Fried foods are hot in nature
8. Ice cold
9. Spicy foods
10. Processed foods that are sour and salty
11. The best way to balance *pitta* is to pour *pitta churna*, *jeerka*, *draksha* over your breakfast, lunch and dinner.

Suitable: Warm or cool, bitter, sweet and astringent tastes. Ghee is better than butter
Unsuitable: steamed hot foods

Pitta persons will have by birth good digestion. They are in the habit of eating innumerable times all the foods, which may, at times disturb and derange the digestion. So one has to be very cautious. The over use of salt, sour and spicy food and in addition to over-eating habit will promote *pitta* increase in the body. *Pitta* has hot properties and hence, it needs cold foods and cold climate. It is better to avoid bitter and astringent tastes in the food.

Pitta

Take: Vegetables, beans, starchy food, grains will cut excessive hunger, carbohydrate diet is good.
Avoid: Hot salty, heavy, fried foods, oily fast foods with sour and salt taste.

Drinks

Take: Cold water, cold soup, salad, bread, butter and low salt. Ghee+warm milk acts as laxative and reduces *pitta*. Avoid ghee if lipids or cholesterol is more add *jerrkadi churna* and garlic to your food.
Avoid: Not iced, hot soup, spicy food, cheese and sour cream, low salt, cocktail with salty snacks, alcohol, dry, salty food, these irritate the stomach. Usually *pitta* imbalance type of person will suffer from heart burn, excessive thirst, irritability and easily quarrelsome.
Take: Cool refreshing food in summer, milk, ice cream, lemon juice, herb tea, mint, and licorice root.

Breakfast

Have: Apple juice is the best, cold cereal, cinnamon and toast.
Avoid: Salt oil and spices, pickles, yogurt, sour, curd, sour cream, vinegar, fermented foods, alcoholic beverages, coffee and orange juice.
Meat: Good fish with little ghee, good chicken, vegetarian diet is good, and taboo fatty meat.

Pitta Fruits

Take	Better to avoid
1. Apple	Banana
2. Orange	Berries
3. Cherries, melon	Sour cherries
4. Coconut, pineapple	Grape fruit
5. Figs	Papaya
6. Prunes	Sour foods
7. Grapes all sweet and preferably ripe	
8. Mangoes	

Vegetables

Take	Better to avoid
1. Asparagus	Onions
2. Mushrooms	Radish
3. Brussels	Tomato
4. Okra	Garlic
5. Sprout	Carrot
6. Peas	
7. Cabbage	
8. Cauliflower	
9. Sweet potato	
10. Cucumber	
11. Leafy vegetables	
12. Green beans	

Kapha pacifying diet

Kapha is more in younger age, especially in children. *Kapha* is present in the chest, throat and lungs and joints. *Kapha* will become aggravated and imbalanced due to eating too much sweets, cold foods and rich nutritious foods. In foreign countries, they prefer to use fats and sugars in their diet. So, they must be overcautious about them. Salt must not be used in excess as it promotes accumulation of fluids in the body, *kapha* in the body leading to oedematous body. A light diet, good for *kapha* in a balanced person. One should take pungent foods, as they protect the appetite and digestion. One must not eat excessively, as it may produce less digestion.

The following types of diets are good for *kapha* constitution:

1. Breakfast with light foods
2. Lightly cooked vegetables and fruits
3. Spicy foods promote digestion, chillies, sesame, cumin, fenugreek and turmeric
4. Hot food
5. Hot apple
6. Pie
7. Bitter, pungent and astringent lettuce
8. Bitter cola
9. Hot water with lemon in the morning
10. Honey
11. Ginger tea
12. Raw fruits
13. Raw vegetables

Foods not good for kapha

1. Cold cream
2. Ice cream
3. Heavy foods
4. Sweet in large quantity
5. Dry foods
6. Meat—pig and beef
7. Sprinkle *kapha churna*, *trikatu churna* over the breakfast, lunch and dinner.

Green Coriander: Any coriander seeds, less black pepper and cumin. All pungent spices and herbs, less of salt, pickles, mustard, sour, salad, vinegar, spicy and condiments.

Grains

Take: White rice, wheat, oats, barley
Avoid: Brown rice, millet, rye, corn

Dairy

Take: Egg white, milk, ghee, butter, ice cream
Avoid: Butter milk, sour cream, yogurt

Meat

Take: Chicken

Avoid: Seafood and red meat

The *kapha* pacifying diet given here is a standard one and so, one must take it to keep the *kapha* in a balanced person, unless otherwise, it is changed by an Ayureda physician. People with a blocked nose over-sleeping with laziness, then, in such person this diet works wonder. One should take hot foods, hot lunch, and warm apple and grilled fish. The cold *kapha* will become less with warm or hot foods. Cooking with grilling, boiling, baking is good for *kapha* in balanced persons.

It is safe to take pungent food before your dinner starts to stimulate digestion, ginger tea or ginger juice works wonder. Coriander tea is also very good, as it reduces *kapha* by its diuretic action.

Pitta

Beans

Take mung beans, chicken peas, soya products and avoid lentils.

Oils

Take: Olive oil, coconut oil, sunflower oil, soya bean oil.
Avoid: Seasame, almond and corn

Nuts and Seeds

Take: Sweet, bitter and astringent in less quantity and cardamom.
Avoid: All spices as they are very hot and aggravate *pitta*.

Pungent foods are not at all good in summer, as they provoke *pitta*. Morning breakfast must be light and not too much for *kapha* in balanced person. One must take hot spiced foods, cold sweet heavy foods are not good. Cold foods such as cold milk and cold juice, as they may create *kapha* production and its imbalance.

Sweets are not good for *kapha* persons, although they like them very much. Honey is the best for *kapha* type of persons. Ayurveda recommends it, but it is not to be taken in large quanitity. A tablespoon a day is safe. It cannot be taken after heating, as it will become unwholesome to body.

Eating too many dairy products—ice cream, butter and cheese are not safe for *kapha* type of persons.

Kapha alleviating foods spices and herbs

Take: Ginger to improve digestion
Avoid: Salt beans. All legumes are good for *kapha* especially kidney beans.

Oils

Take: Sunflower, almond and corn.
Sweeteners

Take: Raw honey is good and heated honey is unwholesome to body.

Seeds and nuts

Take: Sunflower seeds and pumpkin seeds.

Vegetables, raw fruits, salads are very good. Cooked foods are recommended in Ayurveda. One should avoid fried foods as it aggravates *kapha* in the body.

Oils: Groundnut oil, corn oil and sunflower oils are good to be used by *kapha* types of persons. Vegetables must be boiled and taken after little butter is added to it.

One should avoid eating out and in case it cannot be done, and in case they take vegetables with food and not meat in lunch.

One must drink everything hot, hot water and salad. The *kapha churna* (*trikatu churna*) can be sprinkled over lunch before it is consumed to avoid *kapha* production.

Take	Not to take
Apple, dry fruits, apricots, pears pomegranates and figs	Banana, coconut Melons, oranges, papaya, pineapple plums, fresh figs, grapes, grape fruits, sweet and sour fruits

Dairy

Skimmed milk, all except whole milk and eggs

Meat

Chicken, shrimp, turkey	Sea foods and red meat

Grains

Barely buckle Corn whole and millet	Wheat, rice, oats

Vegetables

Take	Avoid
Asparagus, beets	Sweets, vegetable
Brussels, sprouts	Juice, tomato
Cabbage, carrots	Cucumber and sweet
Cauliflower, eggplant	potato
Garlic, green leafy vegetables	
Onions, peas, peppers,	
Potatoes, raddish and sprouts	

Vata

Of foods usually *vata* pacifying diets are good.

1. Oil inunction (abhyanga) to pacify *vata*
2. Medicated anti *vata* enemas.

The patient must take the guidance from an Ayurveda doctor about the nature of constitution, type of diet and ways of taking medicated enemas for Vata to get it balanced at the earliest. It is better to take medicated decoction enema, alternated with oily enemas. The schedule of enemas is 30, 16 and 8 and they are called *karmavasti*, *kalavasti* and *yogavasti*. Any one of these schedules can be tried depending on the severity of the condition and nature of the person. *Vata* alleviating diet is also equally important giving good and early relief to the patient.

There are six properties of drugs

1. Hot or cold to body: Honey is hot and milk is cold, egg is hot and mint is cold.
2. Light or heavy: Milk is light, wheat is heavy, barley is light and pork is heavy.
3. Dry or oily: Honey is dry and coconut is oily.

To balance *pitta*, sweet, sour and salt tastes with hot, heavy and oily materials to be taken.

To balance *pitta*, sweet, bitter and astringent with cold, dry and heavy foods should be taken.

To balance *kapha*, pungent, bitter and astringent foods along with hot, dry and light foods should be taken.

Vata is increased by pungent, bitter and astringent tastes with properties like light, dry and cold.

The *pitta* aggravates due to pungent, sour and salty foods with properties of hot, light and oily.

The *kapha* will be increased due to sweet, sour and salty foods along with properties of cold, oily and heavy. So one has to take food with proper tastes for a particular *dosha*.

Chapter Fourteen

THE DIGESTIVE FIRE (AGNI)
FOR PERFECT DIGESTION AND
ASSIMILATION OF FOOD

If good food is taken at proper times in suitable quantity, then no one will require a doctor. However, since this is not the case, there are diseases like gastric ulcer, duodenal ulcer and peptic ulcer. Ayurveda gives major importance to digestion. Improper digestion leads to many diseases. When digestion is good, then, all the tissues of the body including cells derive proper nutrition and help in the growth of the body.

Doshas and digestion

Ayurveda pleads that persons must consume wholesome food. Three major body types have different digestions.

Vata type of person has a variable, delicate and quick digestion.

Pitta type of person has an intense and strong digestion. That is one can digest even heavy meals.

Kapha type of person has a slow and heavy digestion. It must be improved with by taking ginger tea or coriander with cumin seeds. *Vata dosha* is essentially to have pure blood formation and proper metabolism. The digestion in *vata* type of persons has its ups and downs.

Ayurveda feels that proper digestion leads to proper nutrition to the tissues and proper excretion of excretas called **malas** in Ayurveda. Therefore, it is necessary to balance the *agni* in order to have all the things in a balanced state.

How to kindle the digestive fire

In Ayurveda, *agni* or digestive fire has rhythmic activities. It is necessary to follow the rhythm and to take food in proper quantity at a proper time. If this is not done, it will lead to imbalance in the *agni* and disease will be produced. Villagers are not prone to this type of change of food intake. Therefore, they have no complaint of imbalance of *agni* as well the diseases. This is supreme and laudable, when compared to people living in towns and cities. When food is taken at proper timings, digestion and appetite will be overlapped, leading to the following symptoms.

1. Loss of appetite
2. Constipation or diarrhoea
3. Heart burn (hyperacidity)
4. Burning in stomach
5. Underweight or overweight
6. Sprue
7. Ulcer
8. Irritable colon syndrome
9. Colitis etc.
10. Pain in the abdomen

If the above symptoms appear, then, it is necessary to reset the digestive fire once in 15 days in a month. So also in case of *pitta* types. In *kapha* types it is necessary to reset the *agni* once in 7 days. If you have colitis, diarrhoea, dysentry and ulcer do not reset the *agni* without the doctor's consultation.

It is better to take light diet and take a laxative with castor oil in hot water at bedtime. This is not advisable for persons with ulcers in the stomach and intestines. If they are to be given, then this oil must be mixed with milk. Next day it is better to fast and take liquid diet the entire day. *Vata* and *pitta* types of persons must drink fruit juices diluted with hot water. The juice therapy must be adhered to the entire day. *Kapha* type of persons must drink only hot water. One should not exert too much, but only take rest. It is better to take a light diet, as it is good for the body. Juice therapy is practised by naturopaths of Ayurveda.

On the third day, it is good to take light breakfast, hot water in between and light lunch and a light dinner. One must not drink any alcohol or other soft drinks.

If at all you want to take tea, ginger tea is the best or else tea of coriander with cumin powder. After meals, drink hot water which is digestive and assimilative and increases appetite. Don't take anythings between meals except hot water or ginger tea or coriander tea. The meal must have vegetables, dals and rice. It suits all types of *vata, pitta* and *kapha*. The digestive fire is reset and ready to digest the normal and routine diet. Eating raw vegetables is also a good habit to tone up the system and to keep the body free from diseases.

Coffee, alcohol and salt are best avoided. Coffee is a central nervous stimulant, it stimulates all the organs and temporarily give vigour and exhausts later. So also alcohol. Salt helps to consume more food, more fluids leading to heavy weight and hypertension, later it leads to heart attack.

Ama and digestive fire

Ayurveda postulates that the digestive fire must be in a balanced state and it must be in a position to digest normal food properly at proper time. If the food is cold, old, or stale then the digestive fire will not digest it but such food will create an obstruction to doshas for their proper movement. That stage is called *ama.*

On the other hand if there is too much digestive fire, as soon as food is taken it will be burnt immediately resulting in impaired digestion and the person will become fatigued losing his normal strength.

The digestive fire is in normal balanced state, which is nothing but good health. But, when it is imbalanced leading to *ama*-undigested, polluted food carried to different parts of the body through *doshas* through circulation of blood.

The signs and symptoms of balanced digestive fire:

1. It gives colour to the body
2. Tolerance to exercise
3. Gives good health
4. Ability to carry any weight
5. Ready to do hard labour
6. Strong and sturdy body
7. Ability to eat all types of foods
8. Glowing complexion eye
9. Bright eyes
10. Clear urine
11. Normal faeces without any foul smell
12. No constipation and diarrhoea

Whenever *ama* is produced in the body following early signs and symptoms are noticed:

1. Loss of appetitie
2. Weak digestion
3. Dull eyes and skin
4. Coated tongue
5. Unpleasant taste in the mouth
6. Offensive bad breath
7. Pain in the joints
8. Chronic diarrhoea or constipation.

If digestive fire is balanced and normal, then, automatically the *ama* will be digested and made fit for circulation to nourish the tissues of the body at the quantum level.

Toning up digestive fire

Ayurveda has given innumerable preparation for the improving and toning up of the imbalanced digestive fire to balanced state. They not only improve the appetite, but it also helps in normalising the digestive fire, so as to neutralise the digestive fire in order to neutralise the *ama*. There are some foods, herbs and pungent spices which are suitable in toning up the *agni* to its normal state.

Adraka

Adraka is nothing but wet ginger. It is a potent digestive stimulant. Even dry ginger can be used with great benefit. The small piece of wet ginger is powdered and add two cups of water along with a pinch of coriander and boiled to one cup, which should be taken twice a day, when it is warm, either before or after meals. This must not be used daily. It can be prepared as a tea also. You can also add ginger to boiled vegetables and cakes etc.

In *vata* type of persons salt with ginger is good. But in Pitta type of person one ginger will do, but excess of it provokes *pitta* in the body. *Jeera* (cumin) can be used with benefit.

But in case of *kapha* type of persons ginger tea must be prepared and cooled and taken after adding one teaspoon of honey. Honey must not be used. So also if ginger is used too much, it may cause burning sensation in the stomach and oesophagus. In case this schedule did not give you relief, then, you should consult an Ayurvedic doctor.

Ghee

Ghee is clarified butter. Ghee is the best treatment for *pitta* aggravation or imbalance. Ghee, made of cow's milk is good for health as it does not increase cholesterol in the blood and alleviates *vata*. But, it is not good for *kapha*. Therefore it can be taken after adding bitter and pungent drugs. Ghee can be used in place of oil for cooking. Excess of it is detrimental for the body.

Digestive fire and pungent foods

In ayurveda, there are several spices and herbs which are being used to tone up the imbalanced Agni to normal state. One must not use these things in Pitta type of indigestion, as it aggravates *pitta*.

1. Chitraka (plumbagozyelanica)
2. Pepper (black)
3. Clove
4. Cardamom.

Chitraka root powder is available in pharmacies and it can be used in a minimum quantity in milk or buttermilk after meals. Black pepper powder may also be used with the same benefit for toning up the quality of *agni* to normal. Bitter drugs such as *karela* (bittergourd) are very powerful in increasing the *agni* and also to clear the *ama*. Ginger, clove, black pepper and cinnamom (*twak*) are used to clear the *ama* to balance *agni*. In India, it is the household practice to chew fennel seeds with a pinch of rock salt after meals. This stimulates *agni* and balances it.

A pleasant diet

Happiness is the main thing in our life. Ayurveda advocated many things to make a man happy and healthy. Food is consumed and it goes into several changes and goes to tissues and finally to cells of our body, at the quantum level. The final outcome of food is 'ojas' which is a nectar of food. It gives brightness and shine to the body. It is essential for balancing both body and mind. Mental disorder, anxiety, depression are due to our improper diet.

The satvic diet

There are three types of diet viz *satvic, rajasic* and *tamasic*. At present *satvic* diet details are given. From birth to death satvic type of diet is recommended and is good.

Satvic diet consists of mainly milk and its preparations ghee, butter, rice, sesame, sweets, fruits and fruit juices and all items of sweet preparation. Satvic diet need not be special, but includes fresh, light, soothing and balances of the six tastes with moderate quantity of good water. This is called *satmya ahara* or wholesome food for the mind and body to get good health and long life.

Normal food such as rice, vegetables and fruits, milk in our day to day, is the best. This is also recommended in many diseases, in obese and heart patients.

Milk

Milk is useful for young people and adults. Cow's milk is the best one as it is *satvic*. Milk should be added with one-fourth quantity of water and boiled. It should be preferably used when it is warm in cold season and cold or lukewarm in hot season. It should never be used after keeping in refrigerator. Milk must not be mixed with antagonistic foods—sour, salty and pungent as it produces severe reactions, allergies in the body, itching and allergic rashes on the skin. In sprue it is contraindicated, so also the person with *ama*. *Kapha* type of persons must take a little milk highly diluted. Milk can be mixed with sweet fruits and grains. Milk promotes good health for body and mind, tones up body strength and keeps the mind in tranquility. Butter and cream are really good for such people. It should be added with rock salt or ginger. In cold season, it should be warmed before taking. But in hot weather it can be taken as buttermilk or *lassi* with rose water. This is the best drink for *pitta* type of persons. *Lassi* can be taken after adding a little cardamom and sugar. It keeps your body hot and balanced.

Best rule

Ayurveda method of taking food is very important. The food should be warm and fresh. The time of taking it is also important. It sends signals through saliva and gastric juices to the mind and to the body. The final output of food is ojas, which is the nectar of the food. The smell, sight, touch and hearing send signals to higher level. One should be calm and in good mood while taking food. Any disturbance at the dining table is bound to produce ill effects on digestion, even though one takes homologous food, it will become bad for the body. One must take *satvic* type of food for good nourishment. I have given below fifteen golden rules in order to get maximum benefits from the food you take. Therefore, one must adhere to these rules without fail.

Golden Rules

1. Sit down and eat.
2. Eat in calm atmosphere.
3. Eat when you feel hungry.
4. Do not converse with other's while taking food.
5. Eat in a balanced way, neither too slow nor too fast.
6. Eat only at a specific time.
7. Eat food which is fresh.
8. Eat with six tastes (*shadras*) if possible.
9. Never eat when you are in hurry or excited.
10. Eat properly cooked food.
11. Avoid old stale food.
12. Drink warm water either with meal or aftermeals.
13. Eat only three-fourths of the stomach and leave one quarter empty for early digestion.
14. Drink buttermilk after meals.
15. Sit for some time after meals so that food settles down properly.

Hurry, worry, irritation and excitement will upset digestion. The use of hot water or warm water will aid in the digestion, as warm water itself produces good digestion and assimilation and tastefulness. The use of milk at day time and the use of curd at night is forbidden in Ayurveda for promoting the health of an individual.

TIPS FOR WEIGHT LOSS

An overweight person must follow the following important rules.

1. Eat only when you are hungry.
2. Do not eat carelessly and forcibly.
3. Eat only in time.
4. Eat at regular intervals.
5. Sit and eat preferably in *padmasana* (squatting position).
6. Eat in calm atmosphere.
7. Nothing should be taken in between lunch or dinner.
8. Leave bad habits.
9. Do not overload the stomach.
10. Do not attend to false hunger.
11. Do not eat under pressure of your senses—smell and sight.
12. Eat consciously and judiciously.

Triphala (three fruits) can be taken in a dose 5 to 10 gms with buttermilk. There are some metabolic and hormonal defects, in such conditions a doctor is needed for their rectification. The food should be taken in a good environment. One should not eat when irritated and angry, which will produce enlargement of *pitta* and there by stress is produced. Stress can produce even gastric ulcer. This is seen in experiments on animals and also clinically. The *ojokashaya*-ojodepletion occurs due to irregular food intake and fasting. The good *satvic* diet, pure vegetarian diet is good for producing ojas.

Non-Ojas food

1. Eggs
2. Heavy food
3. Oily food
4. Meat
5. Chicken
6. Fish
7. Cheese
8. Too much salt and sour food
9. Old and stale food
10. Canned food
11. Frozen food

Those who meditate daily must not use garlic, mushroom and onion. The food that is stored in the refrigerator will not be useful for producing ojas.

Most dangerous habits are smoking, drinking alcohol, brown sugar and habit forming drugs like pethidine they must be tabooed, otherwise, it is detrimental to ojas production. Water and air pollution create a tamasic atmosphere, which is not at all good for ojas. Overuse of cold and heavy food produces *kapha* aggravation and later on *ama* production, which is quite opposite to ojas production. Ayurveda has recommended some time honoured regimes for best production of ojas. Fresh food, fruits, vegetables, milk and its products preferably ghee at breakfast, lunch in time. Dinner must be taken in time with your family and friends in a calm atmosphere.

Chapter Fifteen

SIX TASTES (SHADRASAS)

Six Tastes (Shadrasas)

Everything in the world is a medicine, if used in suitable quantity and in specified condition. The world is made of *panchamahabhutas* (pentad) and *shadrasas* (six tastes) are also made up of *panchamahabutas*. The quantum of mechanical body has got a good relevance to *shadrasas*. Our tongue is the better judge of these six *rasas*. viz. sweetness, bitterness and other tastes are all identified by our tongue.

Pungent taste is effective in *kapha* type of persons and sweet taste is useful in *vata* type of persons. Bitter taste in *pitta* type of persons.

Whenever a person feel sweet taste in the tongue, it goes into the entire body including the cells at the quantum level through saliva. The promotion of digestion is made by pungent, sour and salty tastes and the digestion is lowered by cold taste as bitter, astringent and sweet. In foreign countries, red chillies supply vitamin C whereas in India, spices like pepper, serve the same purpose.

Nature and tastes

Nature has given us abundant foods with different tastes viz. lemon is sour, pepper is pungent, milk is sweet and it is wholesome for the body.

Dairy:	Mainly sweet, cheese, sour and astringent
Fruit:	Mainly sweet and astringent, citrus and sour
Nuts:	Grains mainly sweet.
Legumes:	Mainly sweet and astringent spices, anes and herbs
Oils:	Mainly sweet
Meat:	Mainly sweet and astringent
Vegetables:	Mainly sweet and astringent

Majority of food that we consume is sweet and the body is generally is sweet. *Kapha* is the builder of *dhatus* (tissues) of our body. All the structures of our body are made up of mainly *kapha*. The tastes either increase or decrease *doshas* in the body. All oils increase *kapha* and pungent decreases *kapha*. Garlic decreases *kapha* and *vata* but increases *pitta*. Cucumber promotes *kapha* and decreases *pitta*.

In Ayurveda by name, they have not told vitamins, minerals but their main aim is to maintain the decreased doshas to normal and increase doshas to a normal stage or Samyavastha or balanced state.

In India cabbage is generally used as a vegetable and it is scientifically proved that it prevents cancer production. It is used as juice in healing ulcers, although it contains sweet and astringent, dry and cooling. When a person eats food, which will be digested, finally it goes into chemical change called *vipaka*.

There are three *vipakas* viz. sweet and salty tastes, sweet vipaka, sour tastes to pungent vipaka, pungent bitter and astringent tastes to pungent vipaka. So all the six tastes of the food finally after digestion reduced to three *vipakas*.

Now here afterawards we go deep into the details of the tastes.

Sweet (Madura)

Sweet foods are sugar, honey, milk and its products are cream, butter, wheat and rice. Sweet increases *kapha* (excluding honey) and *dosha* lessens *pitta* and *vata*. Sweet rejuvenates the body. It promotes growth of the body. Sweet on taking excess produces *kapha* in the body. It is homologous to the body. All grains, all oils and all meats are considered to be sweet. Both rice and wheat are sweet. The milk products and ghee are also sweet food. Ghee is the specific remedy for *pitta*. Sweet foods are generally soothing to body and it quenches thirst.

When *vata* aggravated, it produces nervousness uncontrolled mood, hurry, worry, excitement, and in such a condition if you take sweet foods or drinks it will cool the Vata and also calm the *pitta*. Excess intake of the sweet brings up heaviness in the body and dullness in the mind and it may also create complications such as diabetes or blood pressure.

Consuming too many sweets can aggravate the *kapha* resulting in indigestion, lethargy, heaviness in the body, balancing and coldness in the body, looseness of body organs and dyspnoea, cough and excessive sleep overweight and excess mucus. In these conditions, it is safe to avoid sweet things. However honey is an exception to this rule. It is the only best medicine for balancing *kapha*.

Salt (Lavana)

Salt decreases *vata*. Salty foods increase *kapha* and *pitta*. Salt stimulates digestion. *Pitta* and digestive fire are one and the same. It provokes appetite. Without salt, either breakfast, lunch or dinner will not be tasty. Salt increases *kapha* and *pitta*. It penetrates into the smallest tissues at the quantum level of the body. It helps to dissolve *kapha* or other substances. It digests *amarasa* (chyle). It is acute in action due to its hot potency. It promotes more digestion leading to obesity and high blood pressure. People suffering from high blood pressure are advised by the doctors to cut salt in their diet schedule. Complete stopping of the salt in the diet is dangerous to body, as it may produce cramps in the muscles, so, it is better for the hypertensive patients to use minimum amount of salt in their diet. High blood pressure is not only due to excess salt in the diet but it is due to derangement of *doshas* in the body.

Excessive use of salt will create an environment, which produces skin diseases and other complications. It is not good to use salt, when either *kapha* or *pitta* diseases are present in the body. So one must use salt in the minimum quantity.

Use of more salts lead to excessive acidity (hyperacidity) ulcers, changes in the blood, skin reactions as blisters and later heart burn and swelling.

Sour (Amlarasa)

Sour foods are; Amalaki (emblica officinalis), lemons, tamarind, cheese, yogurt, vinegar, grapes and tomato. Sour foods decrease *vata* and increase *pitta* and *kapha*. Sour promotes taste in the food. It stimulates digestion, using it continuously, creates more thirst. Sour foods must be given in generalised swellings. The intellect of the *pitta* will be sharpened by the use of sour foods. Too much sour is not good for health. Especially in cheese sourness is due to fermentation. Curd if it is old, will also be sour. Ayurveda prohibits use of fermented sours especially vinegar and alcohol as they are toxic to the body, resulting imbalance of *kapha* and making the tissues lodged with *ama* (undigested particles of food which acts as a poison or toxic to the body).

Bitter (Tiktarasa)

Bitter taste helps in correcting digestion. It is a liver stimulant. It promotes tastes for other tastes like sweet, sour and pungent tastes. It alerts the body through *vata*. People with less digestion can opt for bitter drugs and herbs. Whenever the body is hot and toxic, then the use of bitter herbs works wonders.

Bittergourd, bitter greens, bitter cucumber, spinach, fenugreek and turmeric. Bitter taste decreases *pitta* and *kapha* and increases *vata*.

Whenever we use bitter in large quantity, it aggravates *vata* in the body leading to headache, weight loss, loss of appetite, dry skin and weakness and life will not be happy.

Pungent (Katurasa)

Pungent taste is made up of *agni* and *vayu bhutas*. It has got heating property. It decreases *kapha* and increases *vata* and *pitta*. It keeps the mouth clean and promotes digestion and absorption of food. It not only purifies the blood, but also cures skin diseases. It is light, hot, increases the heat and sweating, fainting, burning sensation in the throat and thirst. The digestion is increased. Sweat, saliva, tears, blood and mucus all start flowing, when pungent taste is used. It is best suited for *kapha* like sinusitis. In cough and other lung troubles, chilli and pepper are used with benefit. Chilli, if eaten raw, may produce burning sensation in the mouth, lips and skin. Pungent foods are not used in case of *vata* or *pitta* imbalance is seen in the body. Pungent foods are: chilli, onion, raddish, garlic, pepper, and asafoetida.

Astringent (Kashaya Rasa)

Astringent taste is cooling. It is a catabolic. It decreases *pitta* and increases *vata*. It has got a sedative action. It produces constipation. It causes constriction of vessels and coagulation of blood. It is dry, cold and cough in its property. Astringent taste makes the mouth dry. It is alkaline in taste, and is opposite to lemons. It is more appetising. It produces tears, sweat and saliva. When it is used in excess, then it produces constipation, dryness in the mouth and distension of abdomen. Astringent food is not advisable for vata imbalance.

Chapter Sixteen

AYURVEDIC EXERCISES:
THE MYTH OF NO PAIN-NO GAIN-NO LOSS

Man's life needs activity. This requires exercise. Activity will make a man hale and healthy. Charaka, a famous Ayurvedic physician, pleads that exercise must be done half of the strength of the individual. The benefits of exercise are as follows:

Lightness, fitness to carry out work, increase digestive fire, defatting of the body and makes the body strong and sturdy and expelling the body impurities.

Types of Exercise

One must do simple exercise. Walking is a fine exercise. One must take light walk after lunch or dinner. Walk will soothe the *vata* in the body. Mild exercise is also good for *pitta*. The *kapha* type of persons need strenuous exercise. The exercise will make the body strong and sturdy. Exercise must be within his limits. Cardiac patients must not exert too much, but they can walk for 1-2 miles per day, either in the morning or in the evening. One need not do exercise to the extent of perspiring. Overdoing will result in the accentuation of *vata* in the body. So one must do exercise to a minimum.

SURYA NAMASKAR (SALUTE THE SUN)

This is a morning exercise. The body organs will be stretched and balanced (1-10 minutes). Yoga stimulates neuromuscular activity. *Pranayama* (balanced breathing),

breathing exercise (5-10 mts). *Pranayama* promotes the intake of oxygen and expels carbondioxide from the body. *Pranayama* regulates the integration of the body and mind. It creates extraordinary balance of the consciousness. It has got too many healing benefits. It not only brings bless, but also joy to the body and pleasantness to mind. For *pitta* constitution left nostril breathing is good. The *kapha* constitution must do breathing in right nostril. It stimulates the energy in the body. Patients/persons of *vata* constitution must breath in alternative nostrils. Yoga prevents many diseases. It helps in health, happiness and long life. It regulates nerves, cleansing, concentration, awakening and contemplation, equilibrium and tranquility of the mind, and leads to peace. Yogic practices help to balance excess stress to normal state. Stress borne or related diseases as asthma, diabetes and obesity are being regulated or maintained to balance them with yoga exercise. Yoga is a science, which helps one to attain *moksha* (salvation). The *sirasasana* (head stand) is contraindicated for *pitta* diseases and in high blood pressure. Continuous shoulder stand is not advisable for *vata* constitution. The Hindus lotus posture must not be conducted for long time for *kapha* constitution, as it directly acts on adrenal glands. Weightlifting and other heavy exercises are recommended for *kapha*. Exercise must be maximum for boys and least for old persons. The old age is the period of *vata* provocation. So, one must not exert too much to avoid *vata* production and aggravation leading to uneasiness and unhappiness.

Exercise not advised

Exercise must not be done immediately after meals, as it lowers the digestive fire. If fluids are taken, then exercise must be done after half an hour. Walking in hot sun will provoke *pitta* in the body. So it must be done in the early morning or late in the evening. Exposing oneself to cold and damp climate, either walking or playing sports in cold climate is not at all good for *vata* and *kapha*. It provokes both *vata* and *kapha* and leads to ill-health and unhappiness.

Exercise scientific analysis

The Myth of No pain-No gain-No loss

Certain changes will occur in organs, when continuous exercises are done. The magnitude of change differs on the type and time of intensive exercise done. Age and heredity play a definite role. There is increase in capillaries in skeletal muscle tissues. The muscles will extract more oxygen and lower lactate from muscle glycogen. The muscle cramps are due to insufficient supply of oxygen. This depends on the mechanism of using oxygen to oxidise glycogen to carbondioxide (CO_2) and water, which yields energy and haemoglobin stored oxygen in red blood corpuscles from blood to the muscle cells. Exercise increases the myoglobin contents in skeletal muscles. There is hundred per cent utilisation of energy of glycogen in the body. This depends on the quantity of carbohydrate food intake. Glycogen is essential for long running i.e. in sports. The enzyme activity in muscles will also be enhanced. The number and size of mitochondria will also increase. There is increased tendency in oxidising fats and carbohydrates in the muscle. The respiratory quotient R.Q is equal to one ($CO_2/O_2=1$). There will be increase in the amount of contractile proteins (actin and myosin) day by day after regular exercise. The production of prostaglandin in the body will be decreased or balanced after exercise. Exercise must be done in a balanced way. It should be done regularly. As it is already stated, activity (exercise) is life and lethargy is next to life. So one should do exercise in moderation, regularly and constantly. This will definitely help in balancing the *doshas*.

Exercise and tridoshas

Exercises are meant for tuning the body. Yogic exercise and meditation not only tune the body, but also tune the mind. All exercises are not difficult to practise. Some may require a teacher or a master for conducting them. Some of the important exercises for doshas are given below:

1. **Menstrual Disorder**—Cobra, plough, sexual, debility backward bend, shoulder stand and plough.
2. **Asthma**-*cobra*—half wheel, bow, fish, shoulder stand and cobra.
3. *Vata* **type back ache**—Knee to chest, half wheel and backward bend.
4. **Sciatica**—Knee to chest, yoga mudra, half wheel and backward bend.
5. **Rheumatoid Arthritis**—Bow, plough, half wheel and backward bend.
6. **Head ache**—Plough, headstand and yoga mudra.
7. **Insomnia**—Cobra, corpse and backward bend.
8. **Depression**—Corpse, lotus, yoga mudra and palmtree.
9. **Constipation**—Yoga mudra, knee to chest, shoulder stand.
10. **Liver disorders**—Hidden lotus, fish and shoulder stand.
11. **Hyperthyrodism**—Ear, knee and shoulder stand.
12. **Hypertension**—Ear, knee and shoulder stand.
13. **Peptic ulcer**—Sheetali (inhaling air through mouth with twisted tongue) and hidden lotus.
14. **Diabetes**—Half wheel, backward bend, forward bend, tiger breath, *pavana muktasana*, boat, fish, *bhujangasana, matsyasana, sarvangasana, nadishuddhi pranayama*, QRT, DRT, 'A' chanting-0 times.

All asanas must be conducted in a calm and quiet atomosphere.

Yogasanas for Vata Dosha

1. **Asthma (Vata)**—Backward bend, plough, knee to chest and corpse
2. **Backache**—Knee to chest, plough and half wheel
3. **Constipation**—*Yogamudra*, knee to chest and shoulder stand
4. **Depression**—*Yogamudra*, Plough, lotus, palmtree and corpse.
5. **Headache**—Head stand, plough and *yogamudra*
6. **Insomnia**—Backward bend, cobra and corpse
7. **Menstrual disorder**—*Yogamudra*, half wheel, plough and cobra
8. **Rheumatoid arthritis**—Half wheel, backward bend, plough and head stand.
9. **Sexual weakness**—Elevated lotus, plough, backward bend and shoulder stand.
10. **Sciatica**—Yogamudra, half wheel, knee to chest, and backward bend.

Yogasana for Pitta Dosha

1. **Anger**—Shoulder stand, half bow, hidden lotus, and corpse.
2. **Colitis**—Bow, boat, fish and ear knee.
3. **Haemorrhoids**—Shoulder stand, fish and bow.
4. **Hypertension**—Quiet breathing, half bow, cobra and shoulder stand.
5. **Hyperthyroidism**—Ear knee and shoulder stand.
6. **Liver diseases**—Hidden lotus, ear knee, shoulder stand and fish.
7. **Migraine**—Fish, shoulder stand and sheetali.
8. **Pepticulcer**—Sheetali and hidden lotus.
9. **Stomatitis**—Sheetali

Yogasanas for Kapha Dosha

1. **Asthma (Kapha)**—Cobra, fish, palmtree, shoulder stand, bow, boat and half wheel.

2. **Bronchitis**—Fish, half wheel, forward and backward bends and head stand.
3. **Chronic intestinal diseases**—Cobra, locust and fish.
4. **Diabetes**—Backward and forward bends, half wheel, fish and boat.
5. **Emphysema**—Shoulder stand and half wheel
6. **Sinusitis and headache**—Fish, head and knee and lion.
7. **Sore throat**—Fish, locust, lion and shoulder stand.

Only few Ayurvedic exercises are dealt here. The remaining *asanas* are to be practised through a master or teacher.

How to perform Surya Namaskara (Sun salute)

Suryanamaskara involves yoga and breathing simultaneously. Thus suryanamaskara is usually done at the time of sunrise or before sunset after passing urine and faeces.

Before starting *surya namaskara*, one must chant the name of sun like ohm hurm, *Suryaya namaha*, while doing. It is very necessary to have breath control while doing *namasakara*. One must expand the chest, while inhaling, contract his abdomen during expiration. There are twelve postures. However here for daily practice all the twelve are given. One has to perform the sun salute one after another with a little break. During that period, one must take a deep breath.

1. Samasthiti: In salutation position, one should stand straight with feet together with his arms folded on front to his chest. You have to expand the left chest and ribs.

2. Tadasana: In raised arm position, one has to extend the arms over his head. Take a deep breath inside. You have to look upwards and breath in till the next pose is started.

Suryanamaskara (step wise postures)

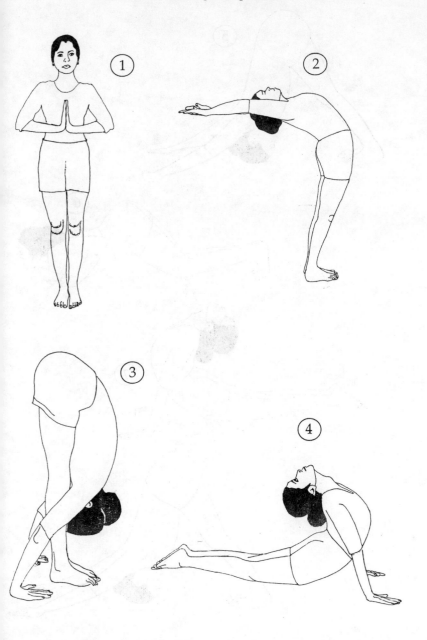

Suryanamaskara (step wise postures)

Suryanamaskara (step wise postures)

3. Uttanasana: Hand to foot position. As soon as you bring down your arms and hands down to foot, you should exhale slowly in this position. Spine and neck will be lengthened and bent in kyphosis way. It is essential not to lock the knees, but to keep shoulders and elbows in a relaxed state.

4. Aswa sanchalanasana: (Equestrian position)—In this posture, it is necessary to extend the left leg and bend the right knee with both your palms rest on the floor in this pose, one must take a deep breath. The spine has to be lifted up and straight in conjunction with his neck and face to the front side.

5. Adhomukha savasana (Mountain position): The exercise is done on exhaling air. One must bring the left leg and right leg together and keep shoulder and hands apart, look through your eyes, your stomach and turn to move the spine upwards to the possible extent and stretch the heels on the floor.

6. Astanga Namaskara (Eight Limbs Position): Feet, knees, arms, chest and chin touch the floor. This is usually done during expiration. Hold your breath for some time and then start.

7. Bhujangasana (Cobra position): On inspiration you have to keep the toes of both the feet on the floor and your two palms apart on the floor and raise your buttocks, head, neck, and chest to the possible extent upwards. Take a deep breath. Expand your chest.

8. Adhomukhasyanasana (Mountain pose): It is nothing but position no 5. Raise hips, buttocks and expire properly and see your abdomen for some time.

9. Aswa sanchalanasana: Is repeated as in No 4.

10. Uttanasana (Hand to foot position): It is repetition of No 3.

11. Tadasana: Raised arm as in Asana no 2

12. Samasthiti: It is a repetition of asana no 1. These twelve postures will complete circle or cycle. Time 10-20 mts. Morning or in the evening on an empty stomach.

The basic Ayurvedic exercises are to be done 10-20 minutes per day. These should be practised preferably in the morning. The simple exercise will make the body warm, increase circulation and blood supply to all the organs and tissues, including ultimately cells at the quantum level of the body. Some of the exercises will create activity in the tissues and promote strength and sturdiness in the tissues expecially muscles, nerves and bones. Some of the exercises will help toning up abdomen muscles, organs and to set in proper digestion. Breathing stimulates lungs and supplies more oxygen to the tissues. The vital capacity of the lungs will be increased, which inhibits any lung diseases and other diseases of the respiratory tract, such as cold, rhinitis, cough and asthma etc. Some of the exercises help in concentration of mind e.g. meditation. Meditation has helped many people including resistant non-curable cancer. To quote an example Smt. Maya Tiwari a famous yogini staying in America, who was suffering from cancer got cured with only meditation, when all other systems of medicine including western medicine failed Your food must be your remedy. Fruits and other raw vegetables in the diet will prevent many diseases including cancer. Excess food is deleterious to body. Eat to live and not live to eat. Nature is the best healer. Eat only when you are hungry.

Pranayama
(A balanced rhythmic breathing)

A balanced rhythmic breathing is called *pranayama*. The person will take air in one nostril and leave in another nostril. This is a type of inhalation and expiration, which is rhythmic in nature. This procedure is nothing but a breathing exercise called *pranayama*. It is a type of neurorespiratory exercise meant for soothing the nervous systems and stimulating lungs activities.

Prebalanced breathing tips

The person who does *pranayama* must keep his mind in tranquility. He should switch off television, radio, tape recorder and cool his body and mind and sit in a *padmasana* style by closing his eyes. One must avoid stress and strain to the body and mind. One should not use any medicines during the balanced breathing. He should pass urine and faeces before starting.

Actual *pranayama* is a balanced breathing technique.

How to do balanced breathing

The patient or a healthy individual who wants to practice balanced breathing must either sit in *padmasana* style or can sit in a chair comfortably closing the eyes in a calm and undisturbed atmosphere.

Anuoloma Viloma Procedure
(A normal breathing pranayama)

One must sit in *padmasana* or *vajrasana* style and keep erect his head, back and waist, close his eyes and expire slowly. Then slowly inhale in both nostrils without loudness.

Later on, the person should exhale outside without noise. The inhalation and exhalation must be equal, about 20 seconds during inspiration the chest and abdomen will be drawn inside. This is done on empty stomach, either in the morning or in the evening. This is repeated from 10 rounds to 30 rounds. One inhale and exhale constitute a round. The lungs, heart and abdomen will be purified. This can be practised up to 3 months continuously. This procedure must be done without any strain or exhaustion, under a qualified Ayurveda physician.

Chandranuloma Pranayama
(Chandranuloma type of balanced breathing)

The inspiration and expiration will take place in left nostrils only; the right nostril will be closed with *nasikamudra*.

Sooryanuloma balanced breathing: In this balanced breathing the inspiration and expiration, take place in the right nostril only. The remaining *niyamas* are as before.

Uses

Cold, cough, sinusitis and pressure headaches will be cured and it promotes digestive fire.

Nadi Shuddhi balanced breathing (Pranayama)

Here the individual breathes from one nostril and expels from the other. The person must sit erect in *padmasana* style and close eyes. The right nostril by right thumb and slowly take deep breath and leave it in the left nostril.

PRANAYAMA

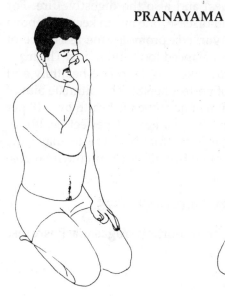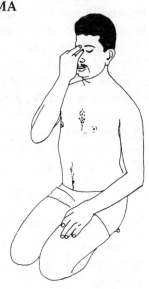

1. Nadishuddhi (Left)   2. Nadishuddhi (Right)

Repeat this on the opposite side of the nostril. That is to say, close upper left nostril and take deep breath from the right nostril and leave it in the left nostril. The inspiration and expiration will be deep gradually in continuous and regular practice. In the beginning from 9 rounds and increase to 30 rounds. This is also done before sunrise and before sunset.

Uses: These are preliminary for real balanced breathing.

This must be continuously practised for 3 to 6 months. The body will be light and the digestive fire will be enhanced and pleasantness of the mind is obtained. In *pranayama,* one need not resort to deep breathing. A normal breathing with rhythmic changes will do and one can get the real benefits of balanced breathings.

Osteoporosis, diabetes and arthritis are all either due to bacteria, virus or fungus. But Ayurveda pleads that the dieases of the body and mind are due to imbalance of doshas, dhatus (tissues) and also the digestive fire. For healthy living, to avoid disease, one has to keep the above in a balanced state. Ayurveda promotes the resistance of the patient through its balanced food and living. The main aim of Ayurveda is to make people to live healthily and happily with a state of perfect health. The ultimate aim of this book is to make a man improve his health by 5-10 per cent in order to attain the real goal of perfect health. In this endeavour an earnest effort is made to make the reader to obtain maximum benefits to attain the final goal of perfect health.

AYURVEDIC EXERCISES

The following are the important Yogasana Postures:

Padmasana
Bhujangasana
Savasana
Mayurasana

Suptavajrasana
Chakrasana
Dhanurasana
Sirasasana
Paschimottanasana
Pavanamuktasana
Bhadrasana
Gomukhasana
Sarvangasana
Siddasana
Kukkutasana
Swasthikasana
Simhasana

ASANAS (YOGIC POSTURES)

PADMASANA

Meditation is done in this posture. The body and mind
will be in peace and in balance. The fat in the thighs will
become less.

Posture: The right knee is folded and the right foot is kept on the left thigh. The two feet and forelegs must be upside and both the legs will be on the sex organs.

Time: 1 minute

BHUJANGASANA

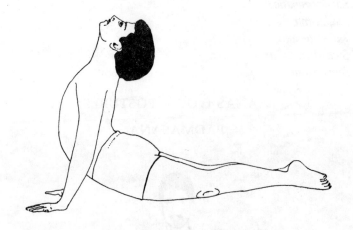

Posture: One must lie down on the bed on the abdomen. Both arms straighten and bring both lower limbs together. The chin must touch the floor. Bring both the arms to the side of the head and the palms must touch the floor.

Bring both the arms to the sides of the last ribs. The arms must touch the body.

Then raise the head and make the upper portion of the umbalicus like snake head and raise it. The body from umbilicus to foot must be on the ground. Then bend the body like a bow.

Time:

Uses

1. The ligament of the back will get strength

2. Backache will become less
3. The fat in the abdomen will become less
4. Respiratory disorders will be relieved

SAVASANA

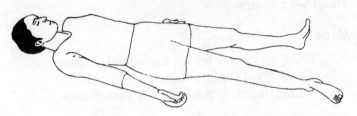

Posture: One should lie down on the floor (bed) with his body fully stretched facing upwards. The legs and arms must be kept apart.

One must concentrate on the head, in between the eyebrows and relax fully.

Time: 1-2 minutes

Uses

1. High blood pressure
2. Good sleep.
3. Keeps the mind and body in tranquility

MAYURASANA

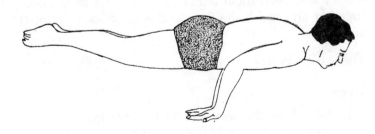

Posture: Follow the three stages of hamsasana. Then keep your body on the floor with your forearms on the ground parallel to ground; you should see forwards and come back to original *samasthiti.*

Time: 1-5 minutes

Uses

1. Good treatment for all abdominal diseases
2. Gives good digestion.
3. Stimulates secretion of abdominal glands.

SUPTAVAJRASANA

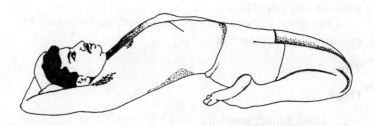

Posture: Lie down on your back by straightening our legs and arms. Make your feet come to back of the body and make your knees come back to the back of hip and waist and keep your entire body weight on it. It is better to make forearms loose and make your hands bend like a scissor and keep them under the head and keep knees together and touch the floor and come back to normal state.

Time: 1-2 minutes

Uses

1. Stimulates the nerves of back and thighs.
2. Relieves stiffness of thighs and back

CHAKRASANA

Posture: One should lie down on his back. Bend your legs and bring them back and bring your hands near your arms and see that your body is on your foot and palms. Take deep inspiration and make your body like an arch for 2 minutes and then come back to original status with expiration.

Uses

1. It gives strength to nerves
2. Useful in diabetes, bronchial

Time: 1 minute

DHANURASANA

Posture: The knees must be net backwards and catch the feet with the palms.

Then raise the head, chest and thighs up and bring the body to a state of Dhanus. The eyes must be upwards. The entire weight of the body must be on the abdomen.

Time: 1-2 minutes

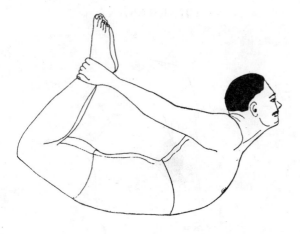

Uses

1. Stomach diseases
2. Indigestion
3. Increases digestive fire

Sirasasana

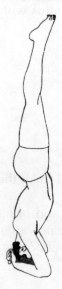

Posture: One must sit on a bed with the knees bent. Then you must fix your both fingers tied together and keep forearm on the ground in a triangular way and keep your head on it. Then, keep your toes on the earth and raise the knee and waist in 90 degrees for about a minute. Then bring your legs to the ground and come to original state of samasthiti.

Time: 1-2 minutes

Uses

1. Increases blood flow to Brain
2. Stimulates pitutary and thyroid glands
3. Orchitis will be relieved.
4. Increases concentration of mind.

Caution: Contraindicated in 1. High blood pressure; 2. Eye diseases.

PASCHIMOTTASANA

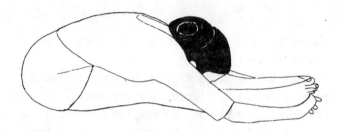

Posture: Straighten the legs and the back and spinal column and sit down. Then raise the arms above so that the arms touch the ears and make arms facing frontside. Take deep inspiration after drawing the upper part of the waist. Then expire slowly, bend the spinal column and make the upper part of body and arms parallel to floor, catch the big toe with index finger.

Bend your back and keep your face in between your knees and your elbows must touch the floor and loosen the muscles of abdomen. Take respite for 2-3 minutes then take inspiration and raise up and come to normal state.

Time: 1-2 minutes

PAVANA MUKTASANA

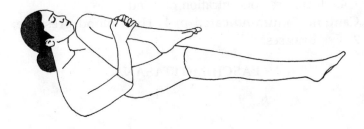

This *asana* is useful in indigestion and constipation. This is done in two stages.

First stage: This is called single foot *pavana muktasana*.

Posture: A patient or a healthy person must lie down in *savasana* posture on the bed, by keeping the knees close to each other and hand must be straightened and kept by the side of the head.

Then right leg must be raised upto 45 degrees from the ground and the left leg must be kept on the ground. One must inspire slowly and once again the right leg must be raised to 90 degrees with full deep inspiration. Then, in the expiration bend the right knee and hold it with fingers and press it to the chest. Afterwards respire normally and keep the chin on the knees and make the left leg move in the half circle with to and fro motion for 5 times. Then he should come back to normal state.

Second Stage: Here both the legs are used and the above procedure is followed by raising both the legs to 45 degrees and later to 90 degrees and the remaining as before, is followed and come back to normal state.

BHADRASANA

Posture: Sit after bending the knees and bend the feet backwards. With two fingers, catch hold of your foot. Your chest, spinal column and head must be in straight line. Inspire and expire for 1 minute.

Time: 1-2 minutes
Uses: It activates thighs, bladder and sexual organs.

GOMUKHASANA

Posture: Sit by bending and keeping the right leg on the left leg. Then left leg must be bent and kept below buttcks. Both hands must be brought back and joined together. The same is repeated with the left leg on the right leg.

Time: 1-2 minutes.

Uses

1. It is a good exercise for spinal cord
2. Useful in abdominal diseases
3. Increases assimitation of food.

SARVANGASANA

Posture: Stand on the back and hold your lower back with two hands. Your head must be on the floor, making your face upwards and both foot and legs be at 90 degrees for 5-8 seconds. Take inspiration and do expiration during this period.

Time: 1-2 minutes

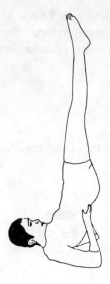

Uses

1. Good exercise to entire body.
2. It promotes health, strength and glamour.

SIDDASANA

Posture: Sit after bending your knees. Make the face, spinal column and neck in straight line. Fold your hands one upon the other and keep it on umbilicus and respire.

Time: 1-2 minutes

Uses

1. Meditation.
2. Saints sitting in this pose meditate.

KUKKUTASANA

Posture: Keep the two hands in between knees and touch the floor for 2-3 minutes.

Time: 1-2 minutes.

Uses

1. The intestines will be purified
2. The Pelic region will be flattened
3. Urogenital diseases will be relieved
4. The *kapha doshas* will be alleviated

SWASTHIKASANA

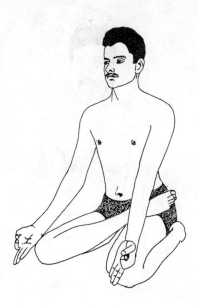

Posture: Sit in *dandasana* posture on a carpet slowly doing expiration. Bend your left leg and keep below the right thigh, and take inspiration. Once again bend your right thigh. During expiration, keeping your hands in chin mudra and close the eyes for 2 minutes. Do meditation; take inspiration and come back to *dandasana* posture.

Time: 1-2 minutes

Uses

1. It dissolves fat in thighs.
2. It relieves stiffness in knees and foot.
3. It promotes intellect in the mind.
4. It increases circulation in the lumbo-sacral region.

SIMHASANA

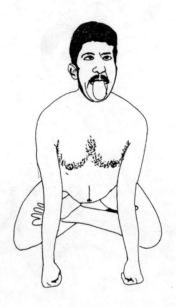

Posture: You bend your knees and keep your legs in Padmasana style. Keep your hands pressing on your knees. Then bend your head and take out your tongue outside your mouth. Make a big sound like a lion.

Time: 1-2 minutes.

Uses

1. Tonsilitis
2. Throat diseases
3. Salivary glands diseases

EPILOGUE

Ayurveda is India's answer to good health. It advocates preventive and curative health care.

Man is a microcosm of the macrocosm of the universe. Everyday some births and deaths take place in this world. It is nature's phenomena. A prominent feature of Ayurveda is that the mind exerts a maximum influence over the body, freedom from diseases and more so a state of balanced living. Ayurveda advocates diet according to one's constitution. It also recommends regularity of intake of food. It pronounces the breathing of good air. If one has to live long, it is necessary that one should have balanced food, balanced digestive fire and balanced tissues. It is also necessary for creating highest state of health, perfect health to have a physical immunity. This will depend upon the consumption of oxygen in proper quantity and quality and expulsion of carbon dioxide in proper quantity from the body. One can enhance his age by eating food as per Ayurveda. He gets diseases due to imbalance of taking food. One must take food according to his body type.

Digestion and Metabolism

Whenever food is taken, it has to be digested and assimilated by the digestive fire and as a result the tissues will get their proper nourishment. The growth of the cells takes place even at the quantum level of the body and mind. The digestive fire must be in balance for the well being of man. So one has to reset the *agni* or digestive fire to a balanced state.

Elimination of waste products

The elimination of waste products from the body is very essential for a healthy living. In this so called over-civilised world, man has no time to attend to his nature's call as urination, defaecation. So with this many diseases will creep in and lead to ill-health. The best way to purify the body and to eliminate the toxins from the quantum level of the body is to adopt purificatory measures like *panchakarma* therapy and meditation therapies to combat mental illness as well as physical illness like cancer and other dreaded diseases. The *satvic* diet and drugs which purify the *doshas* must also adhere to lessen the impurities of the body and mind.

Some diseases can be prevented by following the principles of daily routine and seasonal routine. Some of the diseases are due to bad habits such as drinking of alcohol, tea, coffee, brown sugar and other drugs which are highly toxic and habit forming and dangerous to health and also even to our life. These retard even the age limit.

Our food is flooded with toxic chemicals, pesticides and deodorants and insecticides which are used for the growth of the food and also preservation and disinfection. So man has become poisonous and toxic.

Breathing

Air is as important to our body as food and water. Catch a breath of fresh air whenever you can.

Live in tune with nature

Man is *panchabhoutic*. The world is also made up of *panchabhots*. Man is nothing but an epitome of the universe. So one has to adopt the diurnal routine and seasonal routine, then naturally in the body everything goes on silently and smoothly. This is very essential for the quantum mechanical body and mind. The food intake, its digestion, its assimilation and respiration takes place silently and smoothly. So, one has to plan his life adopting the above routines and also attending to cleansing the body once or twice in a year with pentad of purificatory procedures.

Balancing of mental health

There was a time when the importance of mental health was not given its due place. Ayurveda has given maximum to the proper maintenance of mental health. It has advocated conducting transcendental meditation and the use of primordial sounds, *marma* therapy, *gandharva* music therapy, in order to balance the imbalanced mind. Modern medicine believes that diseases of heart and cancer are due to infection.

Ayurveda, the medical science of life of India, makes the common man to reach the highest goal of perfect health.

To reach deep into insight of consciousness

Ayurveda pleads and practises that one should be in complete harmony and tranquility of mind and body. One will definitely feel taken back and surprised about the word "Perfect Health". But, after going through this book he will find enough details of substantial information and its utility in promoting perfect health. It is opined in Ayurveda that the body is similar to nature, which is living, thinking and breathing organism with super controlling brain. The diseases are man-made as he simply rejects the diurnal and seasonal regimens and the ways of life, in the name of so-called scientific advancement and civilization.

It is late but not too late for human beings to follow the principles of Ayurveda, to live healthily and happily in perfect health for at least one hundred years.

GLOSSARY

Meanings of difficult words quoted in the book

Ayurveda: Science of life, knowledge of life span.

Abhyanga: Oil massage with warm oil.

Ama: Undigested food product, toxic contents present in the cells of the body and mind leading to a disease.

Asana: A yogic posture.

Dhatu: Tissues, seven *dhatus* in the body.

Dinacharya: A diurnal regimen or routine for perfect health.

Doshas: Fundamental principles of the body, when they are in balance, they maintain health of an individual. On their imbalance, they produce diseases.

Gandharva: Ancient tradition of music, employed for bringing mental imbalance to its balance.

Ghee: Clarified butter.

Guna: Natural properties of *vata*, *pitta* and *kapha*, three *gunas* are *satva*, *rajas* and *tamas*. Balance of these produces mental health.

Kapha: One of the three *doshas* necessary for structure and growth of the body.

Maha Bhutas: They are five—earth, water, fire, air and ether—which are present in nature as well as in some proportion in the body.

Marma: A vital point or centre for meeting matter and consciousness. Injury to these causes immediate death.

Nadi: Pulse

Ojas: The final product of tissues of the body and food assimilation.

Panchakarmas: Five procedures of purification. They are emesis, purgation, enema (decoction and oily), blood letting and errhine therapy (*sushruta*).

Pitta: It is nothing but digestive fire and it is necessary for digestion and assimilation of food.

Pragnyaparadha: A mistake in the intellect and consciousness.

Prakriti: It is a general meaning of nature, constitution of an individual, like *vata prakriti*.

Pranayama: A balanced breathing, a type of Ayurvedic respiratory exercises to keep mind's concentration in balance.

Rajas: One of the mental qualities.

Rasas: It is nothing but taste of food. There are six tastes namely sweet, bitter, astringent, salt, pungent and sour.

Rasayana: An ayurvedic tonic for rejuvenation of the body and enhancing age of an individual.

Rishi: A vedic seer dedicated his entire life for the well being of men.

Satva: One of the qualities of mind necessary for keeping one's mental health in balance.

Surya Namaskara: Sun salute, an Ayurvedic yogic exercise.

Tamas: One of the *gunas* of *manas* (mind) which is with inertia.

Vata: One of the three *doshas*, necessary for the entire activity of man even at the quantum level of the body and mind.

Veda: Veda is knowledge of life span and Ayurveda is the *upaveda* of *atharva veda.* .

Vipaka: An end and final product of digestion.

Yoga: A vedic knowledge with many exercises meant for well-being of health of mind and body.

BIBLIOGRAPHY

The ideas expressed in this book are from original Samhitas, in addition to the books quoted in the selected Bibliography, apart from my knowledge and practice of ayurveda, which are highlighted wherever necessary.

A Master Guide to Meditation by Royeugene Davis.

Arogya Prakasha by Vaidya Ramanarayana Sharma.

Astanga Hirdaya by Dr. K.R.S. Murthy, Sootra and Shareerasthana.

Ayurveda and Modern Medicine by Dr. R.D. Leele.

Ayurveda Armotherapy by Light Miller and Brain Miller.

Ayurveda for Health and Family Welfare by Dr. T.L. Devaraj

Ayurveda for Healthy Living by Dr. T.L. Devaraj

Ayurveda Herbal Cure by Dr. T.L. Devaraj

Ayurveda Remedies for Common Diseases by Dr. T.L. Devaraj

Ayurveda Secrets of Health by Maya Tiwari

Ayurveda: The Complete Handbook

Cancer: Causes and Prevention by Dr. Ahuja

Cancer Therapy in Ayurveda by Dr. T.L. Devaraj

Charaka Samhita Chakrapani Teeka, Sootra, Vimana and Chikitsasthanas

Digestion and Metabolism in Ayurveda by Dr. C Dwarkanath

Dravyaguna Vijnana by Dr. N L Bhattacharya

Dravyaguna Vijnana by Prof. P.V. Sharma

Fundamental Principles of Ayurveda Part 1, 2, 3 by Dr. C Dwarakanath

How to Maintain Good Health by Dr. B.M. Hegde

Journey into Consciousness by Charles Breauxt.

Juice Diet for Health Dr. D.K. Gala and others

Madhava Nadana by Prof. K.R. Srikanta M'urthy

Ayurveda: The Computer Handbook

Harita Soamhita: Prathamasthana

Madhava Nadana by Prof. N.L. Upadhyaya

Meditation for Everybody by Pandit Laxmidass

Mental Health in Traditional Medicine by Dr. Balasubramanyam, R.M. Naval

Physiology Volume 1 and 2 by Chatterjee

Prakriti, an Ayurvedic Guide to Health by K.M. Shyamsunder and A.V. Bala Subramanyam

Quantum Healing by Dr. Deepak Chopra

Quantum Questions by Wilbur Ken Boston

Realms of Ayurveda by Pandit Shiva Sharma

Ritucharya, adaptation to the Seasons By A.V. Balasubramanyam, Vaidya Ramesh M Naval

Susrutha Samhita Dalhana, Commentary by Shareerasthana

Textbook of Medicine by Davidson and Price

The Ayurvedic Cook Book by Morning Star and Urmila

Therapeutic Guide to Ayurveda Medicine by Dr. R.R. Pathak

Yoga Deepika by Iyengar

Yoga Mala by Pattabi Jois

Yoga, Vivekananda Yoga Centre

The Panchakarma Treatment of Ayurveda by Dr. T L Devaraj

The Art and Science of Indian Medicine by Gour Srinivasa Murthy